The JESTER AND THE SAGES

MARK TWAIN AND HIS CIRCLE SERIES
TOM QUIRK, EDITOR

UNIVERSITY OF MISSOURI PRESS
COLUMBIA AND LONDON

Forrest G. Robinson
Gabriel Noah Brahm Jr.
Catherine Carlstroem

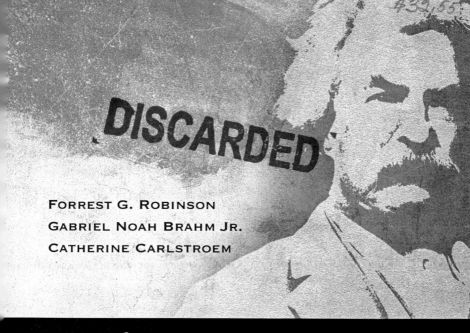

The JESTER AND THE SAGES

MARK TWAIN IN CONVERSATION WITH NIETZSCHE, FREUD, AND MARX

Cataloging-in-Publication data available from the Library of Congress.
ISBN 978-0-8262-1952-7

Design and composition: Jennifer Cropp
Printer and binder: Integrated Book Technology, Inc.
Typefaces: Minion, Copperplate, and Bickham Script

FOR MICHAEL COWAN
LEADER, TEACHER, AMERICAN STUDIES VISIONARY,
AND FRIEND, WITH GREAT RESPECT AND AFFECTION

I have studied the human race with diligence and strong interest all these years in my own person; in myself I find in big or little proportion every quality and every defect that is findable in the mass of the race.

—Mark Twain, *Autobiography*

Contents

Acknowledgments

We could not have completed this work without the invaluable support of many people, including Harry Berger Jr., Stephen J. Burn, James Christianson, John Dizikes, Frank Gravier, David Hoy, Jocelyn Hoy, Peter Kenez, Helene Moglen, Colleen Robinson, Raymond J. Ventre, and John Wilkes.

Gabriel Noah Brahm Jr. and Forrest G. Robinson, "The Jester and the Sage: Twain and Nietzsche," first published in *Nineteenth-Century Literature* 60 (2005): 137–62, is here reprinted in slightly modified form with permission of the University of California Press.

Abbreviations

Complete bibliographic information for the editions of the following works used in this book may be found in the Works Cited.

AMT	*The Autobiography of Mark Twain*
C	*Capital*
CTSSE	*Collected Tales, Sketches, Speeches, and Essays*
CY	*A Connecticut Yankee in King Arthur's Court*
FE	*Following the Equator*
GM	*The Genealogy of Morals*
HF	*Adventures of Huckleberry Finn*
LM	*Life on the Mississippi*
MER	*The Marx-Engels Reader*
MS	*The Mysterious Stranger*
MTHL	*Mark Twain–Howells Letters*
MTN	*Mark Twain's Notebook*
MTP	Mark Twain Papers
PW	*Pudd'nhead Wilson and Those Extraordinary Twins*
RI	*Roughing It*
SE	The Standard Edition of the Complete Psychological Works of Sigmund Freud
TS	*The Adventures of Tom Sawyer*

The JESTER AND THE SAGES

Introduction

FORREST G. ROBINSON

Emerson was right: it was a period in which the mind, like a sharp knife, turned inward on itself. All four of our intellectual protagonists—Nietzsche, Freud, Marx, and Twain—were witness to the massive dereification of Western constructions of religion, morality, history, political economy, and human nature that occurred during the nineteenth century. Rapid change at all levels of experience seemed to undermine the accepted foundations of reality. God was dead. Mankind was more than ever a creature anchored in this world. The old mysteries had become ordinary, but the ordinary had at the same time become mysterious. The world was not so much a divine or natural as a human creation. How, then, and why did humans produce the reality they inhabited and had come to take for granted? The true mystery of religion lay not in its doctrines, but in its human construction and investment with belief. The same could be said of attitudes toward right and wrong, the past, and leading social, political, and economic systems. This general shift in attention toward the human source of prominent beliefs and institutions was at once exhilarating and depressing. Thomas Carlyle reveled in the thought that "this so solid-seeming World" is "but an air-image, our Me the only reality." For Matthew Arnold, by contrast, that same world, no longer uplifted on "the Sea of Faith," had lost its way, and had "really neither joy, nor love, nor light, / Nor certitude, nor peace, nor help for pain."[1]

Whatever the mood, the challenge was to better understand the wellsprings and mechanisms of human creativity. For the great thinkers and writers gathered together in this volume, the search for the vital *human* origins and meaning of such things as religion, myth, history, morality, law and custom, dreams, childhood sexuality, race and slavery, and capital and commodities demonstrated nothing more clearly than the alienation of their creators from themselves and one another. The world, they agreed, is in large degree a fabrication, a human construction wrought by people living in a condition of profound and frequently self-willed blindness to the truth of their condition.

We have placed Mark Twain in "conversation" with Nietzsche, Freud, and Marx not in order to suggest that he was an intellectual of their type. The three Europeans were systematic thinkers engaged in professional, highly focused, lifelong engagements with the leading issues of their time. They were all men who believed in the truth, and who aimed to find it and reveal it to the world. Twain, by comparison, was a writer who worked by fits and starts at a wide array of projects, and who seldom knew where his stories were going until he finished them. Nor is there the slightest suggestion in what follows that Twain was in any way influenced by or significantly influential with his European counterparts. Rather, we have staged these extended comparisons—or "conversations"—between the jester and these three sages to highlight the many and significant ways in which the American humorist's leading questions, ideas, and assumptions overlap with those of his much more solemn and systematic continental contemporaries. The challenge in these chapters has been to look past superficial differences in genre and style to the deeper, often unanticipated intellectual affinities among our four writers.

We readily concede that most of the new light generated by these juxtapositions falls on Twain. Scholars specializing in Nietzsche, Freud, and Marx will find little that is startlingly new in our treatment of their favorite writers, except perhaps that the famous American funny man had quite a good deal in common with them. With all due respect, it is our intention in what follows to deploy consensus readings of the sages as a foundation for expanding the consensus reading of the jester. "The Lincoln of our literature" was a humorist whose gravitas often rose to the level of his moniker. While he was not formally educated, Twain was a lively autodidact of broad interests, great intellectual acuity, powerful imagination, penetrating intuition, and urgent moral promptings. These qualities are everywhere at large in his writing, though their force is often obscured by the disjunctive trend in his narratives and the incendiary brilliance of his humor.

Readers may wonder why we decided to place this particular group of European thinkers in conversation with the American humorist. There were a number of factors at play in our decision. All of our sages are figures of undoubted authority and influence who continue to enjoy large audiences, and whose diverse areas of interest open numerous avenues into the life and work of their New World counterpart. At the same time, none of the three was well known to Twain, and there is scant if any evidence of significant influence. This consideration was important to us because we wanted to emphasize the striking independence and fecundity of Twain's intellectual life, not his debts to major contemporaries. It is for this reason that we decided not to include a chapter on Darwin, whose writings—as Sherwood Cummings has so ably demonstrated—were well known to the American and directly influenced several of his books.[2]

We are hardly alone in turning our attention to the engaged and often troubled intellectual "behind" the celebrated comedian. We recognize with gratitude that our efforts run parallel to those of other scholars who have in recent years enriched our understanding of Mark Twain by drawing his very real—if rarely systematic or fully developed—intellectual engagements into bolder relief. This enterprise has gravitated to the later, often-neglected "dark" decades of the writer's life, and it has yielded a portrait of the artist more varied and generally more somber than its predecessors'. Justin Kaplan, James M. Cox, Roger B. Salomon, and Hamlin Hill figure prominently in the vital early stages of this now-discernible trend. Prominent more-recent voices include

Lawrence I. Berkove, Harold K. Bush Jr., Gregg Camfield, Joseph Csicsila, Sherwood Cummings, Carl Dolmetsch, Shelley Fisher Fishkin, Susan Gillman, Randall Knoper, Peter Messent, K. Patrick Ober, Tom Quirk, and Chad Rohman. We are greatly pleased to be able to supplement the work of these esteemed scholars.

Our chapter on Twain and Nietzsche foregrounds their common defiance of the moral and religious truisms of their time. Both craved freedom—the more complete, the better. They were at one in their longing for a simpler, more primitive experience of life in which humans are free to follow their natural instincts and desires unencumbered by the oppressive constraints of Christian civilization. They associated such immunity to the blight of modern religious morality with animals, children, and great warriors. Nietzsche's critical reflections on slave morality, *ressentiment,* and the tyranny of conscience have their counterpart in Twain's contempt for the Moral Sense, which thrives on a factitious distinction between good and evil, and which ushers moral and psychological devastation into the lives of its deluded proponents. Remorselessly punishing guilt is the disease of modern man; blissful (or ecstatic) surrender to what comes naturally is the antidote. The medicine afforded Twain no permanent cure, though the failure of the remedy hardly diminished his struggle against the disease. His thinking agreed with Nietzsche's that the culture of guilt is reinforced by the fear of righteous disapproval of peers, and that the pitiable result is a craven retreat to bad-faith moral evasion and bland conformity.

Freud was also concerned with guilt and conscience, or what he came to view as the destructive hegemony of the superego. This link between the American humorist and the Viennese doctor was one strand among several in their shared, lifelong fascination with the mysteries of the human mind: with the formative influence of childhood, with mesmerism, mental telepathy, repression, multiple personalities, hypnotism, dreams, twinning and the uncanny, and above all else, with the unconscious. They both believed that the unnatural rigors of Christian morality make a misery of civilized existence. But neither had any illusions about the ultimate pleasure of life; indeed, both equated pleasure with a decrease in stimulation tending toward the complete release from the stresses of consciousness into blissful oblivion. They were closely attentive to the play of the unconscious in art. Both looked to dreams as a window on the human psyche, and to the unconscious as a realm of freedom from restraint in the expression of the deepest human wishes. Freud erected a myth of familial conflict between rebellious sons and their fathers, while Twain came back again and again to stories of houses divided by warring brothers.

Our comparative chapter on Twain and Marx bears witness to sharply divergent personal involvements in major social and economic questions of mutual concern. Where Marx was direct and unambiguous in his analysis of the ills of capitalism, Twain was torn between incompatible perspectives that made him highly vulnerable to contradiction. Despite significant differences in their views of human nature, history, and the likely prospects for progress, Twain and Marx were both profoundly disturbed by the economic and social injustice in the world as they found it, most especially as it was manifest in the gulf opened by industrial capitalism between the privileged elite of property owners and the vast class of property-less workers. They were moralists impatient with conventional morality, committed to freeing ordinary people from the illusions that kept them in chains. Both condemned the alliance of the state with the bourgeoisie in the two entities' narrowly self-interested support of the economic status quo. They agreed that religion was a force for ill, not least as it joined ranks with the social and economic elites and promoted the ideological half-truths that reconciled workers to lives of squalor.

As the excitement over the recent publication of his autobiography shows, Twain's stature as an artist and national icon is more secure than ever. The alignment of his books on the same shelf with those of Nietzsche, Freud, and Marx will do little one way or the other to change that. But if these essays help to enrich the understanding of the most popular of American canonical authors, if they focus attention on some of the deeper and darker shades of his intellectual makeup, and thereby supplement our appreciation of the forces driving his creativity and the dynamics of his humor, then one of our principal goals will have been reached. We trust as well that our comparative approach will open fresh perspectives on Twain's writing, drawing scholars and general readers alike along previously unexplored avenues of interpretation. For example, the chapter on Nietzsche and Twain brings important but underemphasized dimensions of the humorist's moral thought—his impatience with conventional understandings of good and evil, his craving for release from unnatural civilized restraint, and his searching reflections on guilt—boldly into focus. *The Genealogy of Morals*, we find, yields especially rich insights when studied comparatively with "The Facts Concerning the Recent Carnival of Crime in Connecticut," "My First Lie and How I Got Out of It," and *The Mysterious Stranger*. The comparative treatment of Twain and Freud throws new light on the novelist's tendency to equate freedom with the reduction of mental stimulation—most especially as it takes rise from the conscience—and to equate complete freedom with oblivion. Such equations, developed at length in *Beyond the Pleasure Principle* and *Civilization and Its Discontents*, resonate powerfully with Huck Finn's craving for the ease, comfort, and satisfaction of life aboard the raft, his obsession with death, and his concluding decision to light out on his own ahead of the next wave of civilization. Finally, the comparison with Marx serves to highlight the complexity of the American writer's views on social and economic injustice, his grasp of their ideological underpinnings, and his gathering sense that the possession of property has its foundation in a history, usually denied and concealed, of theft, conquest, enslavement, and murder. When read against the analytical background of *Capital*, several of Twain's major works, including *Roughing It*, *Tom Sawyer*, *Huckleberry Finn*, *A Connecticut Yankee in King Arthur's Court*, and *Following the Equator* take on a special, specifically American urgency of implication.

NOTES

Because we anticipate that some members of our audience will be specialists interested in only one chapter of this book, we have taken steps to ensure that each chapter is complete and freestanding. As the inevitable result, there is in succeeding chapters some duplication of argument and evidence. We trust that readers will understand.

1. Thomas Carlyle, *Sartor Resartus,* ed. Kerry McSweeney and Peter Sabor (New York: Oxford University Press, 1987), 44; Matthew Arnold, "Dover Beach," in *The Poems of Matthew Arnold,* ed. Kenneth Allott (New York: Barnes and Noble, 1965), 242.

2. Sherwood Cummings, *Mark Twain and Science: Adventures of a Mind* (Baton Rouge: Louisiana State University Press, 1988), 33–34, 57–58, 170–71, 181–83.

One

TWAIN AND NIETZSCHE

GABRIEL NOAH BRAHM JR.
AND FORREST G. ROBINSON

In early July, 1906, Mark Twain's secretary, Isabel Lyon, was advised by a friend to read Nietzsche's *Thus Spoke Zarathustra*. A week later, on July 13, she exclaimed in her diary, "'Zarathustra' has arrived!" Lyon was immediately taken with the book. "Here I am," she reported the next day, "reading 'Thus spoke Zarathustra' and I do not pretend to be qualified to say how wonderful I find it." Her enthusiasm seems to have spread through the household. A month later, on August 8, Lyon records that "the King [her nickname for Mark Twain] wanted to see my Zarathustra. It pained me to give him up, but I did it. And after the King had looked through it he said, 'Oh damn Nietzsche! He couldn't write a lucid sentence to save his soul.'" Lyon goes on, "Somehow I am glad he doesn't like Zarathustra. Very, very glad—but I shall be able to quote some passages to him—some telling passages—for Nietzsche is too much like himself."[1]

Twain's initial response to Nietzsche, it seems clear, was like Freud's, a retreat from familiarity prompted by the glimpse of a spirit "too much like himself" for comfort.[2] A kindred ambivalence surfaced two days later. "The King says, 'Damn Nietzsche' when I offer a quotation for the King's approval. First he damns—but then he approves with his head on one side in his quaint listening attitude." Lyon continued for several months to plumb the depth of the analogy between the two writers, and by early autumn fell to praising her employer for his defiance of the "criminal" Christian God, "the one who made man so that he has to sin and can't help himself." "Like Nietzsche," she continues, Twain's "cry was not one of weak pity for the human, but of fierce condemnation for the creator of the devils that war within the human breast."[3] Nor, quite evidently—and quite despite his gruff dismissals—was the humorist unmindful of his kinship with the infamous German. In an autobiographical dictation on September 4, 1907, he declares that he has not read Nietzsche, but acknowledges at the same time a certain familiarity and sympathy with the German's ideas. "Nietzsche published his book," Twain declares, "and was at once pronounced crazy by the world—by a world which included tens of thousands of bright, sane men who believed exactly as Nietzsche believed but concealed the fact and scoffed at Nietzsche" (MTP).

While it is perfectly clear that Mark Twain was aware of *Thus Spoke Zarathustra*, there is no evidence that he more than glanced at the book, or that its author was a direct influence in any of his writings. Twain's philosophical ideas had pretty much jelled by the time Isabel Lyon brought Nietzsche to his attention. Her acute perception of a likeness between the two writers was undoubtedly triggered by her familiarity with *What Is Man?* the Socratic dialogue and "Gospel of Self" that Twain was preparing for publication in the spring of 1906. *What Is Man?* gives voice to ideas that had been smoldering for decades and that Twain felt compelled to write down and preserve for posterity. But because the book was relentless in its exposure of human selfishness, he elected to issue it in a small and anonymous edition for private circulation. Lyon, who helped with the proofreading, was an enthusiastic admirer of the subversive sentiments on display in *What Is Man?* It is "so absorbingly interesting," she wrote in her diary, "that once you begin a galley, you can't stop until you've read all the batch. And Mr. Clemens does like it so much! It is his pet book."[4] It is a reasonable surmise, then, that Lyon's enthusiasm for *Thus Spoke Zarathustra*, which she received just a few weeks later, was fueled by its perceived intellectual kinship with her employer's defiant little tract.

Others have followed Lyon in glimpsing an affinity between Twain and Nietzsche. Carl Dolmetsch finds no evidence of direct influence, but observes nonetheless that Nietzsche's ideas were "commonplaces" of the "European intellectual milieu" that Twain entered during his residence in Vienna in 1897–1899, when he first set to work on *What Is Man?* Jennifer L. Zaccara is equally measured in what she describes as Twain's "acceptance of a Nietzschean worldview." It is a virtual certainty, she argues, that the American would have become aware of Nietzsche's nihilism during his stay in Vienna. She is quick to add, however, that "Twain came to a nihilistic vision on his own . . . and that he nurtured this dark view of the world over the years" before the Austrian sojourn.[5] We concur entirely with Zaccara that Twain's intellectual debt to Nietzsche was small, involving little more than confirmation of an enduring trend. At the same time, however, we have found that the similarities between the thought of the two writers are closer and much more numerous than the scholars have recognized. The link that Isabel Lyon glimpsed in 1906, and that Dolmetsch and Zaccara briefly elaborate, is one matching element among many others in the separate but parallel ideas of Nietzsche and Twain on the human condition. Indeed, we suspect that had the two writers met and compared views, they would have experienced a stunning shock of recognition.[6]

Though we assign Nietzsche's work to philosophy and Twain's to literature, both writers were brilliant psychologists with a common and compelling interest in the submerged wellsprings of human behavior. Both were maverick moralists given to immoralist masquerades. Both shared Freud's interest in the unconscious, his inclination to trace modern discontent to the tyranny of suppressed or unacknowledged psychic phenomena, and his generally dark prognosis for civilization at the end of the nineteenth century. Indeed, both were at times disposed to view the world as a madhouse. "The earth," Nietzsche exclaims in *The Genealogy of Morals*, "has been a lunatic asylum for too long" (*GM* 227). Twain's Satan takes the same view, writing back to hell that earth "is a strange place, an extraordinary place, and interesting. There is nothing resembling it at home. The people are all insane."[7] But even as they condemned the modern world, both writers tended to exempt humans from responsibility for their condition. The belief in free will, they agreed, was as groundless as the unseen engines of behavior were real. Nietzsche was persuaded of what he described as "man's complete lack of responsibility for his behavior and for his nature,"[8] while Twain never wearied of blaming God or temperament or circumstance for human degradation. "Why do you reproach yourself?" asks Satan. "You did not make yourself; how then are you to blame?" (*MS* 250). The writers were alike, then, in mingling contempt for humans with a belief in their essential innocence.

The madness of the world was most broadly manifest for Nietzsche and Twain in hegemonic Christian civilization. "I can think of no development that has had a more pernicious effect upon the health of the race," the German declares, than the Christian ascetic ideal. "It may be called, without exaggeration, the supreme disaster in the history of European man's health" (*GM* 280). For his part, Mark Twain took the view that there had never been "a stupider religion" than Christianity,[9] that in time it would be recognized "that all the competent killers are Christian" (*MS* 137), and that modern Christendom might best be imagined as "a majestic matron, in flowing robes drenched with blood. On her head, a golden crown of thorns; impaled on spines, the bleeding heads of patriots who died for their countries— Boers, Boxers, Filipinos; . . . Protruding from [her] pocket, [a] bottle labeled 'We bring you the Blessings of Civilization. Necklace—handcuffs and a burglar's jimmy.'"[10] Though his indictment was broader than Nietzsche's, Twain certainly shared the philosopher's view that Christian civilization was most lethal in its infliction of psychological suffering on individual believers.

He returned to this point on numerous occasions, but nowhere more memorably than in *The Mysterious Stranger*, where Satan inveighs against

> a God who could make good children as easily as bad, yet preferred to make bad ones; who could have made every one of them happy, yet never made a single happy one; . . . who gave his angels painless lives, yet cursed his other children with biting miseries and maladies of mind and body; who mouths justice, and invented hell—mouths mercy, and invented hell—mouths Golden Rules, and forgiveness multiplied by seventy times seven, and invented hell; . . . who created man without invitation, then tries to shuffle the responsibility for man's acts upon man, instead of honorably placing it where it belongs, upon himself; and finally, with altogether divine obtuseness, invites this poor abused slave to worship him! (*MS* 404–5)

Nietzsche traces the malaise of modernity back to the ancient origins of what he describes as "slave morality." "All truly noble morality," he writes, "grows out of triumphant self-affirmation. Slave ethics, on the other hand, begins by saying *no* to an 'outside,' an 'other,' a non-self, and that *no* is its creative act" (*GM* 170–71). Such *ressentiment*, closely linked for Nietzsche with Christianity, arose historically out of the hatred of the weak for the strong, of the slave for the master. But because their survival necessitated the repression of the craving for power and revenge, the weak internalized their aggressive instincts. The result was an intensification of consciousness, and with it the development of a punishing conscience. Having turned his desire for outward revenge inward upon himself, the now "guilt-ridden man seized upon religion in order to exacerbate his self-torment to the utmost" (*GM* 226). To the very considerable extent that slave morality achieved hegemony in the Christian West, revenge upon the masters, now themselves humbled and disciplined by the new dispensation, was achieved. But the victory, earned at the price of surrender to "the most terrible sickness that has wasted man thus far," was of course no victory at all. Driven by furtive resentment of all that is noble and free, and inwardly tormented by remorseless guilt, humankind was in thrall to a parched, punishing regime. "What a mad, unhappy animal is man!" Nietzsche declares (*GM* 226).[11]

It is perhaps the most painful irony of all that humans are innocent of the terrible guilt unleashed upon them by their proud but utterly groundless morality of good and evil. "My demand upon the philosopher is known," Nietzsche proclaims, "that he take his stand *beyond* good and evil and leave the illusion of moral judgment *beneath* himself."[12] Where there is no possibility of wrong there can be no real guilt, only its crippling illusion. "The bite of conscience," he insists, "like the bite of a dog into a stone, is a stupidity."[13] The historical assault on the free outward play of instinct was for Nietzsche the commencement of all our mortal woe. "Every naturalism in morality," he argues, "every healthy morality—is dominated by an instinct of life. . . . *Anti-natural* morality—that is, almost every morality which has so far been taught, revered, and preached—turns, conversely, *against* the instincts of life." More directly and succinctly still: "All that is good is instinct—and hence easy, necessary, free."[14]

Who that has read Mark Twain's most famous novel can fail to be reminded of Huck's words at the end of chapter 18, when he has escaped the murderous, moralizing Christian civilization along the shore and rejoined his friend Jim on the raft in the middle of wide Mississippi? "We said there warn't no home like a raft, after all. Other places do seem so cramped up and smothery, but a raft don't. You feel mighty free and easy and comfortable on a raft" (*HF* 155). The fugitive boy's feelings directly reflect those of his maker, who enjoyed drifting down great rivers precisely because of the peace of mind—and most especially the freedom from nagging guilt—brought on by the journey. Ten days of rafting on the Rhone in 1891, Twain wrote to his friend, Joseph Twichell, left his "conscience in a state of coma, and lazy comfort, and solid happiness. In fact there's *nothing* that's so lovely."[15] A kindred sentiment surfaces to view in the title of Twain's unpublished manuscript *The Innocents Adrift*, a section of which was posthumously published in *Europe and Elsewhere*. "To glide down the stream in an open boat, moved by the current only," and thereby to experience "a strange absence of the sense of sin, and the stranger absence of the desire to commit it,"[16] was for Twain the height of attainable mortal bliss.

But of course neither the writer nor his most famous protagonist were able for very long to avoid the shore, and the inevitable anguish awaiting them there. Huck's subsequent "adventures" present constant and baffling challenges to his sense of right and wrong. At one crucial juncture, when his instinctive loyalty to Jim draws him into conflict with conventional values, he rounds toward a Nietzschean perspective on morality. "Well, then, says I, what's the use you learning to do right, when it's troublesome to do right and ain't no trouble to do wrong, and the wages is just the same? I was stuck. I couldn't answer that. So I reckoned I wouldn't bother no more about it, but after this always do whichever came handiest at the time" (*HF* 128). Despite his resolve, Huck underestimates the subtle and tenacious authority of the moral scheme in which he is entangled. In time, however, when complete disenchantment finally sets in, he decides to sever all ties with Christian civilization. "I reckon I got to light out for the Territory ahead of the rest," he reflects, "because aunt Sally she's going to adopt me and sivilize me and I can't stand it. I been there before" (*HF* 362).

Twain and Huck are closely akin to Nietzsche in their approval of instinct, of all that is easy, natural, and free, and in their corresponding impatience with Christian civilization and its irrational tyranny of conscience. During his long, varied, and often tumultuous life, guilt was the humorist's special curse. "The Facts Concerning the Recent Carnival of Crime in Connecticut," in which Twain claims to have murdered his odious conscience, makes comedy of what was in fact a permanent blight on his spirit. "Remorse was always [his] surest punishment," observes Albert Bigelow Paine. "To his last days on earth he never outgrew its pangs."[17] The moral burden was compounded by his perverse habit of blaming himself on occasions when others were the victims of suffering for which he had no direct responsibility. Years after her father's death, Clara Clemens paused to comment on this dominant strain in his makeup. "If on any occasion," she observed, "he could manage to trace the cause of someone's mishap to something he himself had done or said, no one could persuade him that he was mistaken. Self-condemnation was the natural turn for his mind to take, yet often he accused himself of having inflicted pain or trouble when the true cause was far removed from himself."[18] Twain's moral anguish takes clear if oblique expression in *A Connecticut Yankee in King Arthur's Court*. "If I had the remaking of man," muses Hank Morgan, "he wouldn't have any conscience. It is one of the most disagreeable things connected with a person; and although it certainly does a great deal of good, it cannot be said to pay, in the long run; it would be much better to have less good and more comfort" (*CY* 219).

Like Nietzsche, Twain was increasingly persuaded of both the groundlessness and the destructiveness of the conventional Christian distinction between good and evil. During the last decade or so of his life, his views coalesced in a bitter attack on what he called "the Moral Sense." Satan, the "hero" of *The Mysterious Stranger*, speaks quite clearly and directly for Twain in excoriating humanity as a

> paltry race—always lying, always claiming virtues which it hasn't got. . . . Inspired by that mongrel Moral Sense of his! A Sense whose function is to distinguish between right and wrong, with liberty to choose which of them he will do. Now what advantage can he get out of that? He is always choosing, and in nine cases out of ten he prefers the wrong. There shouldn't *be* any wrong; and without the Moral Sense there *couldn't* be any. And yet he is such an unreasonable creature that he is not able to perceive that the Moral Sense degrades him to the bottom layer of animated beings and is a shameful possession. (*MS* 72–73)[19]

Here, then, is Twain's version of Nietzsche's slave morality. The distinction between good and evil is without foundation, and those who proudly make choices based upon it are the contemptible victims of a delusion that enslaves them to the darkness in themselves and to the tyranny of conscience. True, Twain set forth no genealogy of moral decline from past freedom to present bondage; rather, he was inclined to characterize human nature as unchanging in its perverse tilt toward iniquity. Hopelessly alienated from the blissful freedom of their instinctive lives, humans surrender all too readily to the destructive allure of the Moral Sense. "Civilization *is* Repression," Lyon protested to her diary in 1905, reporting on a conversation with her famous employer; "you have to jam down out of sight the action of the strongest laws of your being and the great cry of truth."[20] Nietzsche, the passionate advocate of what he regarded as a natural, healthy morality, firmly grounded in the instinct of life, could hardly have disagreed. Indeed, he would have gone further still to insist that "man, with his need for self-torture . . . invented bad conscience in order to hurt himself" (*GM* 225–26). Twain advances the identical view in "The Facts Concerning the Recent Carnival of Crime in Connecticut," where his sadistic conscience declares, "It is my *business*—and my joy—to make you repent of *every*thing you do."[21]

Nietzsche and Twain were also at one in the belief that contemporary Christian civilization, ensnared in an unnatural morality enforced by predatory conscience, required for its creation and maintenance a culture based in fear and immersed in lies. Again, Twain's analysis is comparatively scattered and unsystematic, giving scant attention, for example, to Nietzsche's pivotal notion of *ressentiment*. But the writers were nonetheless in agreement on key essentials. "The refinement of morality increases together with the refinement of fear," the German noted in 1880. "Today the fear of disagreeable feelings in other people is almost the strongest of our own disagreeable feelings."[22] Twain was equally impressed with the human craving for self-approval, and with the resulting fear of disapproval from others, which in combination form a virtually irresistible drive toward conformity. Such is the unequivocal message of much of Twain's late writing, most directly expressed perhaps in "Corn-Pone Opinions," which takes as its text the sage declaration of a young slave: "You tell me whar a man gits his corn-pone, en I'll tell you what his 'pinions is." "Broadly speaking," Twain observes, "there are none but corn-pone opinions. And broadly speaking, Corn-Pone stands for Self-Approval. Self-approval is acquired mainly from the approval of other people. The result is Conformity."[23]

But of course conformity to a slave morality could be achieved only at the price of widespread individual and collective surrender to varieties of evasion, disavowal, deceit, and self-deception—to a culture, in short, of lies. Nietzsche's "contempt for evasive falsification," observes Philippa Foot, was "one of the strongest things in him."[24] His feelings found their focus in the devious dynamics of *ressentiment*, the "art of simulation" which "reaches its peak" in the bitter struggle of the slave majority against the noble master class: "Here deception, flattery, lying and cheating, talking behind the back, posing, living in borrowed splendor, being masked, the disguise of convention, acting a role before others and before oneself—in short, the constant fluttering around the single flame of vanity is so much the rule and the law that almost nothing is more incomprehensible than how an honest and pure urge for truth could make its appearance among men." In a civilization given over almost entirely to slavish *ressentiment*, Nietzsche bitterly complained, "to be truthful means using the customary metaphors—in moral terms: the obligation to lie according to a fixed convention, to lie herd-like in a style obligatory for all."[25]

Mark Twain took a strikingly similar view of both the vast domain and cultural dynamics of deception. Indeed, we cannot too much emphasize the importance of the lie in the work of both writers, who shared nothing so much perhaps as the sense that humankind is in permanent retreat from a true reckoning with its own reality. "There are those who scoff at the schoolboy, calling him frivolous and shallow," Twain reflects. "Yet it was the schoolboy who said 'Faith is believing what you know ain't so'" (*FE* 132). In the same vein, Nietzsche observes: "'Faith' means not *wanting* to know what is true."[26] In the view of Satan—in *The Mysterious Stranger*—the human "race lived a life of continuous and uninterrupted self-deception" (164). In Twain's work more generally, as in Nietzsche's, pervasive deceit is invariably bound up with moral evasion. As illustration we need look no further than *Huckleberry Finn*, *Pudd'nhead Wilson*, "The Man That Corrupted Hadleyburg," and *The Mysterious Stranger*. But Twain is most direct and emphatic on this issue in two essays devoted specifically to the subject of lying. In the first, "On the Decay of the Art of Lying," which he presented at a club in Hartford in 1882, he ruminates briefly and archly on the axiom that "lying is universal—we *all* do it; we all *must* do it. Therefore, the wise thing is for us diligently to train ourselves to lie thoughtfully, judiciously."[27] In "My First Lie and How I Got Out of It," published nearly twenty years later, in 1899, his tone is much more sober and deliberate. Once again, he states unequivocally that "all people are liars from the cradle onward, without exception." Deceitfulness is the very essence of human nature, and it is so by virtue of an "eternal law." Since man "didn't invent the law," he is not responsible for its effects; "it is merely his business to obey it and keep still." This act of concealment, this master lie about the universal sway of deceitfulness, he goes on, is "the lie of silent assertion; we can tell it without saying a word, and we all do."[28]

The silent acquiescence in known deceit is integral to what we have elsewhere defined as "bad faith," the reciprocal deception of self and other in the denial of departures from leading public values.[29] Bad faith as it appears in Twain's work bears the clear implication that humans will sometimes permit what they cannot approve so long as their complicity is submerged in a larger, tacit consensus. For Nietzsche, a person in thrall to *ressentiment* "is neither truthful nor ingenuous nor honest and forthright with himself" (*GM* 172). Such a person will cling to Christian faith, which for the philosopher involves "wishing *not* to see something that one does see; wishing not to see something *as* one sees it. . . . The most common lie is that with which one lies to oneself."[30] In similar fashion, Twain views epidemic self-deception as a leading symptom of the disease of modern Christian civilization. "In the magnitude of its territorial spread," he observes of the lie of silent assertion, "it is one of the most majestic lies that the civilizations make it their sacred and anxious care to guard and watch and propagate." The silence in fact speaks volumes about the ubiquitous influence of the Moral Sense, the perverse human gravitation to evil, and the subsequent bad-faith denial of complicity in gross injustice. "It would not be possible," Twain continues, "for a humane and intelligent person to invent a rational excuse for slavery; yet you will remember that in the early days of the emancipation agitation in the North the agitators got but small help or countenance from any one. Argue and plead as they might, they could not break the universal stillness that reigned, from pulpit and press all the way down to the bottom of society—the clammy stillness created and maintained by the lie of silent assertion—the silent assertion that there wasn't anything going on in which humane and intelligent people were interested." People were witness to a species of the same mute moral evasiveness, he adds, in the response to the Dreyfus case in France, and in the refusal among many in England to acknowledge the injustice of the war in South Africa. "The silent colossal National Lie," he concludes, "is the support and confederate of all the tyrannies and shams and inequalities and unfairnesses that afflict the peoples" of the world.[31]

Nietzsche and Twain are thus at one on many important issues. They agree on the madness of modern Christian civilization. They agree as well that the disease has its wellspring in the displacement of healthy human instinct by a groundless and pathological moral culture of good and evil—a culture feeding on fear, fostering massive and oppressive guilt, and dependent for its maintenance on the proliferation of lies. To be sure, their ideas on these matters do not overlap in all details. As we shall see, Twain knew something of *ressentiment*, but it was not as central or developed in his thinking as it was in Nietzsche's. And though both writers emphasize the role of lies in modern life, Nietzsche highlights the self-deception requisite to faith in the dominant moral system itself, while Twain is equally attentive to bad-faith evasions of the injustices suffered by the victims of civilization. Despite these differences, however, the parallels in the thought of these maverick contemporaries are numerous and remarkably close.

Nor have we exhausted the fertile ground for comparison of Nietzsche and Twain. The striking intersection of ideas at the core of their analysis of modern civilization forms a kind of center from which an array of cognate perspectives may be seen to arise. Because they were sharply attentive to the contradictions in human experience, both writers gravitated to aphorisms—brief, pithy, paradoxical utterances often featuring unanticipated turnings and juxtapositions. Wrote Nietzsche: "The greatest giver of alms is cowardice"; "Beware of the good and the just! They like to crucify those who invent their own virtue for themselves."[32] And Twain: "There are several good protections against temptations, but the surest is cowardice"; "The principal difference between a cat and a lie is that the cat has only nine lives" (FE 324, 622). Like Nietzsche, Twain was a pioneer of modern prose characterized by abrupt transitions, discontinuity, and fragmentation. For both, contradiction and paradox, everywhere manifest in conventional morality, were the inevitable offspring of faith in a nonexistent God. Hardly immune to contradiction themselves, both alternated between contempt for their kind and a forgiving sense of human innocence. Both regarded the idea of free will as an illusion;[33] both strongly inclined to determinism.[34] Neither put much faith in democracy, established judicial systems, or the idea of human equality. They agreed on the role of the unconscious in human motivation, and shared a belief in the analytic significance of dreams.[35] Both recognized a potent, often unintentional autobiographical impulse in their writing. "Yes," Twain acknowledged in 1886, "the truth is, my books are simply autobiographies,"[36] while Nietzsche described his work as "the confession of its originator, and a species of involuntary and unconscious auto-biography."[37] Both yearned after the imagined bliss of life in earlier, less "civilized" circumstances, and both acknowledged a powerful craving for oblivion. Neither believed that most humans would choose to live their lives over again.[38]

While it could hardly be argued that our principals were animated by a sanguine surplus, there are nonetheless several overlapping strands of optimism in their thought. Both prescribed laughter as a cure for the spiritual ailments of the modern world. "Not by wrath does one kill but by laughter," advises Zarathustra. "Come, let us kill the spirit of gravity." And again: "Laughter I have pronounced holy; you higher men, *learn* to laugh!"[39] Satan, Zarathustra's counterpart in *The Mysterious Stranger*, offers virtually the same advice. The human race, he insists, "has unquestionably one really effective weapon—laughter. Power, Money, Persuasion, Supplication, Persecution—these can lift at a colossal humbug,—push it a little—crowd it a little—weaken it a little, century by century: but only Laughter can blow it to rags and atoms at a blast. Against the assault of Laughter nothing can stand" (*MS* 165–66). Laughter emerges for both writers from the interplay between happy illusions and painful realities. For Nietzsche, laughter is linked to *amor fati*, the wise yea-sayer's embrace of all of life, suffering and loss included, as elements necessary to the unfolding of destiny. For Twain, by contrast, laughter tends to take its rise not from the transcendence of naive illusions, but rather from the discovery of their pervasive authority among hopelessly gullible human beings. His humor is powerfully driven by the spirit of the tall tale, a calculated assault on audience credulity.[40]

The philosopher and the humorist were also at one in affirming that humans have the potential, little recognized or developed, to create and to re-create themselves and their world. "When the Christian crusaders in the East happened upon the invincible Society of Assassins," Nietzsche relates, "they must have got some hint of the slogan reserved for the highest ranks, which ran, 'Nothing is true; everything is permitted.' Here we have real freedom, for the notion of truth itself has been disposed of" (*GM* 287). During a long, tumultuous career, Twain made intellectual gestures along similar lines, and may be said to have embodied the self- and world-creating spirit that Nietzsche celebrates. But it was not until the last, often dark years of his life that the humorist fully articulated his own version of ultimate human freedom. Once again, he spoke through Satan. "My mind *creates!*" he exults. "Creates anything it desires—and in a moment." The doctrine takes an even more radical turn at the very end of *The Mysterious Stranger*, where Satan declares, "*Nothing* exists; all is a dream. . . . *Nothing exists save empty space—and you!*" God, good and evil, the terrible burden of guilt—"these things are all impossible," he insists, "except in a dream." Satan is careful to highlight the liberating significance of his message—"I your poor servant have revealed you to yourself and set you free"— and adds that the key to contentment in solitary, infinite space is simply to "dream other dreams, and better!" (*MS* 114, 404–5).

Our writers were also strikingly at one in their esteem for animals, children, and selected warriors and aristocrats, whom they regarded as exemplary of the honesty and freedom wanting in most adults. "The creation of freedom for oneself and for new creation—that is within the power of the lion," argues Zarathustra. "The creation of freedom for oneself and a sacred 'No' even to duty—for that, my brothers, the lion is needed." But strength for resistance is itself not enough, he continues, which is why "the preying lion [must] still become a child." For "the child is innocence and forgetting, a new beginning, a game, a self-propelled wheel, a first movement, a sacred 'Yes.'"[41] Here is humanity freed from the corrupting accretions of history and civilization, fresh and joyous in its instinctive embrace of a brave, new world. Robert C. Solomon describes Nietzsche as "a misanthrope who translated his disgust with humanity as he found it into an inspiring portrait of humanity (or superhumanity) as it once was and again may be." This idealized figure, Solomon adds, is possessed of a "master morality" that is "not only good but in some sense more natural, healthier, and truer to our ideal nature" than the slave morality that has displaced it.[42] Animals and children living outside the dark circle of good and evil, and therefore free of the master morality, have their direct counterparts for Nietzsche in warriors and aristocrats equally removed in spirit from modern decadence. "Among the noble," observes the philosopher, "mental acuteness always tends slightly to suggest luxury and overrefinement. The fact is that with them it is much less important than is the perfect functioning of the ruling, unconscious instincts or even a certain temerity to follow sudden impulses, court danger, or indulge spurts of violent rage, love, worship, gratitude, or vengeance. . . . It is a sign of strong, rich temperaments that they cannot for long take seriously their enemies, their misfortunes, their *misdeeds*." The master morality flourishes among those whose limited and undeveloped intellects scarcely influence or impede a natural impetuosity at once robust and heedless of consequences. Because "such characters have in them an excess of plastic curative power, and also a power of oblivion" (*GM* 172–73), they are free in a mindless sort of way to follow the promptings of instinct unencumbered by artificial considerations of right and wrong. Warriors, Nietzsche believed, were supremely gifted with this highest form of moral and physical health. "The human being who has *become free*," he declares boldly, "spits on the contemptible type of well-being dreamed of by shopkeepers, Christians, cows, females, Englishmen, and other democrats. The free man is a *warrior*."[43]

Twain entertained an array of strikingly similar ideas, though with him they were characteristically more moderate and unsystematic. Like Nietzsche, he looked upon the childhood of mankind as an age comparable in its blissful freedom and moral perfection to that enjoyed by animals. "Adam was perfect before he got the Moral Sense," Twain declares, and "imperfect as soon as he got it. In the one case he *couldn't* do wrong, in the other he could. Adam fell; the other animals have not fallen. By the supreme verdict of God they are *morally perfect*."[44] It is little wonder, in this light, that Twain looked back on his own early days with such aching nostalgia. Once childhood has passed, he wrote in 1900 to the widow of his old friend Will Bowen, "life is a drudge, & indeed a sham. A sham, & likewise a failure. . . . I should greatly like to re-live my youth, & then get drowned. I should like to call back Will Bowen & John Garth & the others, & live the life, & be as we were, & make holiday until 15, then all drown together."[45] Little wonder as well that when they play, Twain's fictional boys make violent war and indulge in "orgies," all with unreflecting, animal indifference to adult moral consequence.

The aristocrats and warriors that Hank Morgan encounters in *A Connecticut Yankee in King Arthur's Court* are themselves childlike in the free, impulsive play of their instincts and in their immunity to guilt. "They were a childlike and innocent lot," he reflects. "It was hard to associate them with anything cruel or dreadful; and yet they dealt in tales of blood and suffering with a guileless relish that made me almost forget to shudder" (*CY* 39). King Arthur is so completely and unselfconsciously the noble warrior that he is unable to simulate the outward bearing of a slave, even when his life depends upon it. "Your soldierly stride, your lordly port—these will not do," Hank insists. "You stand too straight, your looks are too high, too confident. The cares of a kingdom do not stoop the shoulders, they do not droop the chin, they do not depress the high level of the eye-glance, they do not put doubt and fear in the heart and hang out the signs of them in slouching body and unsure step. It is the sordid cares of the lowly born that do these things" (*CY* 361). The king is admirable in Hank's eyes, as we must imagine he was in Twain's, because his rather dim, unreflecting self-assurance renders him invulnerable to the oppressive doubts that weigh on those cursed with more active minds. Hank accords the king the same respect that Satan shows for animals in *The Mysterious Stranger*. Satan angrily rejects the use of the word "brutal" to describe human cruelty. "You should not insult the brutes by such a misuse of that word," he insists. "No brute ever does a cruel thing—that is the monopoly of the snob with the Moral Sense. When a brute inflicts pain he does it innocently. . . . He does not inflict pain for the pleasure of inflicting it—only man does that" (*MS* 72).

Viewed from this perspective, Twain's hero worship of Ulysses S. Grant and Joan of Arc makes especially good sense. In his eyes, the general and the maiden were moral paragons whose childlike innocence was directly linked to their extraordinary military prowess. Both were instinctive warriors whose valor and stoicism arose unreflectingly from the simple integrity of their natures. Grant, Twain observes admiringly, "was no namby-pamby fool, he was all *man*—all over—rounded and complete."[46] But he was this precisely because he was also "the most simple-hearted of all men,"[47] an innocent who expressed himself with "frankness and a child-like naivety."[48] Like Grant, Joan is the composite of all noble virtue. She is truthful and steadfast and of dauntless courage. Her military genius is entirely natural—"born in her," we are assured—and she fights with "an intuition which could not err." In battle she is relentless: "It is storm! storm! storm! and still storm! storm! storm! and forever storm! storm! storm! hunt the enemy to his hole, then turn her French hurricanes loose and carry him by storm!" And yet at the core of Joan's fierce martial instinct is unblemished innocence and simplicity. She is "that wonderful child"; she is "perfectly frank and childlike"; she engages others in a manner that is "fresh and free, sincere and honest, and unmarred by timorous self-watching and constraint."[49]

Odd as it may seem, Twain's Satan is cut from some of the same cloth as the heroic American general and the warlike French maiden. Creatures of his divine make, Satan declares, "cannot do wrong; neither have we any disposition to do it, for we do not know what it is." His military might and moral innocence are simultaneously on display when he effortlessly destroys a castle and its five hundred occupants, an exploit that leaves him "full of bubbling spirits, and as gay as if this were a wedding instead of a fiendish massacre." He is noble and aristocratic in all things: charming, resourceful, radiant with health and vigor, self-confident, and "surpassingly handsome—handsome beyond imagination!" But above all else, Satan's radical innocence exempts him from the sway of conventional morality, thereby freeing him to follow his instincts beyond good and evil, wherever they may lead. "*We* have no morals," he insists proudly; "the angels have none; morals are for the impure; we have no principles, those are chains for men. . . . We wear no chains, we cannot abide them; we have no home, no prison, the universe is our province; we do not know time, we do not know space—we live, and love, and labor, and enjoy, fifty years in an hour, while you are sleeping" (*MS* 49, 52, 176, 370).

The potent innocence shared by Grant, Joan, and Satan is uncommon by any standard, not least of all perhaps because none of the three is distinguished by what we may think of as intellectual virtue. None of them is at all thoughtful or reflective; none displays the slightest tendency toward ratiocination. This is of course because they are actors, not thinkers; so comprehensive is their innocence, their transcendence of all considerations of good and evil, that they are free—as animals are free—of the necessity to engage in moral reflection. Thus with them there is no gap between thought and deed, between instinctive impulse and action. This divorce of rational deliberation from true moral freedom is, in Nietzsche and in Twain, the manifestation of a more general distrust of the human intellect. For both writers, conscious thought is not only in thrall to the tyranny of deceit and self-deception at large in modern civilization, but also in league with it. The mind is home not to a mechanically precise Enlightenment calculator, but rather to a ragged throng of competing impulses, most of them weak, selfish, and prone to all manner of deceit and self-deception. Behaving thoughtfully was for our paired writers the furthest thing from behaving naturally or truthfully or well. "The development of consciousness, the 'spirit,'" Nietzsche declared, "is for us nothing less than the symptom of the relative imperfection of the organism; it means trying, groping, blundering—an exertion which uses up an unnecessary amount of nervous energy. We deny that anything can be done perfectly as long as it is still done consciously."[50] The historical emergence of human reflective power was simultaneous, in the philosopher's view, with the onset of bad conscience and *ressentiment*, when, for the first time, members of the species "were forced to think, deduce, calculate, weigh cause and effect—unhappy people, reduced to their weakest, most fallible organ, their consciousness!" (*GM* 217).

We need look no further than *Huckleberry Finn* to find answering sentiments in the work of Mark Twain. Huck is morally and emotionally on firm ground so long as he yields to the promptings of his heart. Almost invariably, however, when he pauses to reflect on his relationship with Jim, his instinctive sense of justice is clouded by the encroaching racial perversities of his culture. At such moments, the innocent, unreflecting child is overtaken by the corrupting consciousness of an adult. "Can a beast do wrong?" Twain asks in *What Is Man?* "No," comes the reply, "for it is without consciousness." Further on he observes, "Morally and in all other details but one—intellect—man is away below the other animals. God does not value intellect."[51]

The shared suspicion of human consciousness, like so many kindred points of comparison between Nietzsche and Twain, is widely on display, sometimes directly, sometimes more obliquely, in the work of both writers. It is precisely because the "evidence" is so widely broadcast that our survey of the striking similarities between the philosopher and the humorist has been rather dispersed and piecemeal: narrower, more detailed attention to individual works would have failed to suggest the true latitude of common ground. We hasten to add, however, that it is possible to examine many of the key correspondences between Nietzsche and Twain in a few, well-selected texts. Indeed, in Nietzsche's case, one text, *The Genealogy of Morals*, a seminal work on knowledge, morality, conscience, *ressentiment*, and human nature generally, will serve very well as a basis for comparative study. On Twain's side, the most relevant texts are the late *What Is Man?* a Socratic dialogue on human nature, and *The Mysterious Stranger*, an unfinished philosophical novel. "The Facts Concerning the Recent Carnival of Crime in Connecticut," the essays on lying, and such social writings as "Corn-Pone Opinions," "The United States of Lyncherdom," and "To the Person Sitting in Darkness" are also germane, as they speak to the discontents of modern civilization. Among Twain's major fictions, *Huckleberry Finn* and *Pudd'nhead Wilson* are of undoubted interest, though none perhaps is more Nietzschean in its social and psychological analysis than *Tom Sawyer*, a novel that dramatizes the complex interplay between childhood innocence and adult "bad faith" in everyday life on the American frontier.

The hero of the story, young Tom, is a gifted leader who succeeds where most adults fail because of his intuitive, unselfconscious mastery and manipulation of the psychological forces—fear, envy, and bad conscience prominent among them—at large beneath the surface of life in his community. Tom lies without guilt, rushes headlong into imagined battles without fear, triumphs over Injun Joe, the embodied village nightmare, and enjoys youthful immunity to the moral malaise that afflicts his neighbors. In his intuitive social command, heroic sangfroid, and unshakable self-confidence, Tom is a boyish exemplar of the Nietzschean master morality. He is a "born leader" who never doubts his right or his ability to take charge, and who never fails. He succeeds because he follows his instincts, and he heeds the rules only when it is convenient to do so. "He would be President, yet," his neighbors predict, "if he escaped hanging" (*TS* 189).

Tom's principal adversary, his half brother, Sid, is even more clearly at home in the Nietzschean moral universe. Sid is a quiet boy; he is socially inept, but secretly ambitious for distinction. It follows almost inevitably that he is bitterly jealous of his handsome, outgoing, extravagantly resourceful sibling, who achieves without apparent effort all that Sid craves but can never call his own. Sid is driven by the compulsive resistance to an envied "other" that Nietzsche describes as the defining characteristic of "slave ethics." True to type, Sid is utterly, perversely dependent on Tom; his only action is reaction to what he hates. He spies on Tom and tattles to their aunt Polly; he is a resolute killjoy, and contrives whenever possible to subvert his rival's grand schemes; he lies awake at night listening for damaging revelations in his sleeping half brother's disjointed mutterings. He is a consummate embodiment in literature of *ressentiment*, the hallmark feature of Nietzsche's moral psychology. Indeed, nothing in *Tom Sawyer* describes Sid nearly so well as these words from *The Genealogy of Morals*: "His soul squints; his mind loves hide-outs, secret paths, and back doors; everything that is hidden seems to him his own world, his security, his comfort; he is expert in silence, in long memory, [and] in waiting" (*GM* 172).

As their lives wore on, Nietzsche and Twain grew increasingly emphatic in their dissent from the reigning optimism about progress and civilization. Both lost their faith in language and truth and the stability of human identity; and both, in turn, paid a heavy price for their defiance of the comforting certitudes shared by the majority gathered along the cultural mainstream. Their writing became more edgy and private, even obscure; much went unpublished. Their interior lives were equally unsettled. Both suffered alienation from family and friends; both endured isolation and loneliness; both knew something of madness; and both craved oblivion. We are moved by the spectacle of such misery to fantasize a meeting between these aging twins of genius. We like to imagine that they would have been quick to identify each other as kindred spirits, and that understanding and warm trust would have issued from their genial shock of recognition. A happy fiction! In fact, of course, for Nietzsche as for Twain, the only real relief for what ailed them lay on the other side of the grave.

NOTES

We are grateful to David Hoy and Jocelyn Hoy of the University of California, Santa Cruz for timely guidance on key philosophical issues.

1. Isabel Lyon, Diary, MTP.

2. Freud wrote in 1931: "I rejected the study of Nietzsche although—no, because—it was plain that I would find insights in him very similar to psychoanalytic ones" (in Peter Gay, *Freud: A Life for Our Time* [New York: Norton, 1988], 46).

3. Lyon, Diary, August 10 and October 12, 1906, MTP. "This morning," Lyon reports on August 27, "I said to the King, 'Nietzsche says—' 'Oh, damn Nietzsche.' 'But Mr. Clemens, Nietzsche calls the acts of God, "divine kicks".' 'Hurrah for Nietzsche!' the King shouted, and slapped his leg hard."

4. Lyon, Diary, May 24, 1906, MTP.

5. Carl Dolmetsch, *"Our Famous Guest": Mark Twain in Vienna* (Athens: University of Georgia Press, 1992), 228; Jennifer L. Zaccara, "Mark Twain, Isabel Lyon, and the 'Talking Cure,'" in *Constructing Mark Twain*, ed. Laura E. Skandera Trombley and Michael Kiskis (Columbia: University of Missouri Press, 2001), 120, 115.

6. Nietzsche was also well aware of Mark Twain. For example, in 1879 he offered to send his friend Franz Overbeck a copy of *The Adventures of Tom Sawyer*. See *The Portable Nietzsche*, ed. Walter Kaufmann (New York: Viking, 1968), 73.

7. Mark Twain, "Letters from the Earth," in *What Is Man? and Other Philosophical Writings*, ed. Paul Baender, 405.

8. Friedrich Nietzsche, *Human, All Too Human*, 1:107, as quoted and discussed in Philippa Foot, "Nietzsche's Immoralism," in *Nietzsche, Genealogy, Morality*, ed. Richard Schacht (Berkeley: University of California Press, 1994), 10–11.

9. Mark Twain, autobiographical dictation, June 22, 1906, MTP.

10. Mark Twain, "The Stupendous Procession," in *Mark Twain's Fables of Man*, ed. John S. Tuckey (Berkeley: University of California Press, 1972), 405.

11. We are indebted here to Jörg Salaquarda's "Nietzsche and the Judaeo-Christian Tradition," in *The Cambridge Companion to Nietzsche*, ed. Bernd Magnus and Kathleen M. Higgins (New York: Cambridge University Press, 1996), 90–118.

12. Friedrich Nietzsche, *Twilight of the Idols*, in *The Portable Nietzsche*, 501.

13. Friedrich Nietzsche, *The Wanderer and His Shadow*, in *The Portable Nietzsche*, 68.

14. Nietzsche, *Twilight of the Idols*, in *The Portable Nietzsche*, 489–90, 494.

15. Samuel Clemens to Joseph Twichell, in *Mark Twain's Letters*, ed. Albert Bigelow Paine, 2 vols. (New York: Harper and Brothers, 1917), 2:558.

16. Mark Twain, "Down the Rhone," in *Europe and Elsewhere, The Writings of Mark Twain*, def. ed., 37 vols. (New York: Harper and Brothers, 1922–1925), 29:129, 139.

17. Albert Bigelow Paine, *Mark Twain: A Biography*, 4 vols., in *The Writings of Mark Twain* (New York: Gabriel Wells, 1923), 1:65.

18. Clara Clemens, *My Father, Mark Twain* (New York: Harper and Brothers, 1931), 6–7.

19. See also *What Is Man?* 86: "Since the Moral Sense has but the one office, the one capacity—to enable man to do wrong—it is plainly without value to him."

20. Lyon, Diary, September 23, 1905, MTP.

21. Mark Twain, "The Facts Concerning the Recent Carnival of Crime in Connecticut," in *CTSSE*, 1:654.

22. Nietzsche, *The Portable Nietzsche*, 75.

23. Mark Twain, "Corn-Pone Opinions," in *CTSSE*, 2:507, 510.

24. Foot, "Nietzsche's Immoralism," in *Nietzsche, Genealogy, Morality*, 4.

25. Friedrich Nietzsche, "Of Truth and Lie in an Extra-Moral Sense," in *The Portable Nietzsche*, 43, 47.

26. Friedrich Nietzsche, *The Antichrist*, in *The Portable Nietzsche*, 635.

27. Mark Twain, "On the Decay of the Art of Lying," in *CTSSE*, 1:828–29.

28. Mark Twain, "My First Lie and How I Got Out of It," in *CTSSE*, 2:439–40.

29. See Forrest G. Robinson, *In Bad Faith: The Dynamics of Deception in Mark Twain's America* (Cambridge: Harvard University Press, 1986).

30. Nietzsche, *The Antichrist*, in *The Portable Nietzsche*, 635, 640.

31. Twain, "My First Lie and How I Got Out of It," in *CTSSE*, 2:440, 446.

32. Nietzsche, *The Wanderer and His Shadow, Thus Spoke Zarathustra,* in *The Portable Nietzsche,* 70, 176.

33. In his *Introduction to Nietzsche as Political Thinker* (New York: Cambridge University Press, 1994), Keith Ansell-Pearson ascribes to Nietzsche "the radical view that notions of free will, of the subject and the 'soul', are fictions which have been invented by weak and oppressed people" in order to "hold the strong responsible for their actions and make them feel guilty about their strength (you are evil to be strong) and, at the same time, [to] glorify their own lack of strength as a condition of inner freedom" (18). So construed, free will is integral to *ressentiment.*

34. "Man the machine," Twain wrote, "man, the impersonal engine. Whatsoever a man is, is due to his *make,* and to the *influences* brought to bear upon it by his heredities, his habitat, his associations" (*What Is Man?* 128). According to Brian Leiter, Nietzsche held the closely related view that "human beings lack free will, and are determined to do what they do, and believe what they believe, by largely *natural* facts about their physiology and their psychological drives" (*Nietzsche on Morality* [New York: Routledge, 2002], 71–72).

35. See Ronald Hayman, *Nietzsche: A Critical Life* (New York: Oxford University Press, 1980), 226–27; Foot, "Nietzsche's Immoralism," 10; *Mark Twain's Notebook,* ed. Albert Bigelow Paine (New York: Harper and Brothers, 1935), 348–52.

36. Mark Twain to Miss Kate Staples, October 8, 1886, MTP.

37. Friedrich Nietzsche, *Beyond Good and Evil,* trans. Helen Zimmern (Buffalo, NY: Prometheus Books, 1989), 10.

38. Many Nietzsche scholars interpret the doctrine of eternal recurrence as an implicit posing of the question whether life is worth repeating. See Bernd Magnus and Kathleen M. Higgins, "Nietzsche's Works and Their Themes," in *The Cambridge Companion to Nietzsche,* 37–38. Twain's response to the question was perfectly unequivocal: "There has never been an intelligent person of the age of sixty who would consent to live his life over again" ("Letters from the Earth," in *What Is Man?* 428).

39. Nietzsche, *Thus Spoke Zarathustra,* in *The Portable Nietzsche,* 153, 407–8.

40. Ibid., 407–8. On *amor fati,* see *Ecce Homo,* "Why I Am So Clever," sec. 10, and *The Gay Science,* sec. 276.

41. Nietzsche, *Thus Spoke Zarathustra*, in *The Portable Nietzsche*, 139.

42. Robert C. Solomon, "One Hundred Years of *Ressentiment*: Nietzsche's *Genealogy of Morals*," in *Nietzsche, Genealogy, Morality*, 99.

43. Nietzsche, *Twilight of the Idols*, in *The Portable Nietzsche*, 542.

44. Twain, *What Is Man?* 474. Cf. "Letters from the Earth," in *What Is Man?* 403–4.

45. Mark Twain to "Mrs. Bowen," June 6, 1900, MTP.

46. *Mark Twain's Letters*, ed. Paine, 2:460.

47. *Mark Twain's Autobiography*, ed. Albert Bigelow Paine, 2 vols., in *The Writings of Mark Twain* (New York: Gabriel Wells, 1925), 1:38.

48. *Mark Twain's Letters*, ed. Paine, 2:459.

49. Mark Twain, *Personal Recollections of Joan of Arc* (New York: Oxford University Press, 1996), 235, 230, 461, 123.

50. Nietzsche, *The Antichrist*, in *The Portable Nietzsche*, 581.

51. Twain, *What Is Man?* 469, 475.

Two

TWAIN AND FREUD

FORREST G. ROBINSON

"I had not read Nietzsche or Ibsen, nor any other philosopher," Mark Twain insisted in 1907, for "I knew I should not find in any philosophy a single thought which had not passed through my own head."[1] Though Freud was much readier to acknowledge the impress of philosophers on his thought, he shared the American humorist's aversion to Nietszche, fearing that he "would find insights in him very similar to psychoanalytic ones."[2] Yet Twain and Freud knew even less about one another than either knew about the celebrated author of _Thus Spoke Zarathustra_. True, Carl Dolmetsch advances circumstantial evidence to suggest that they "probably met more than once" during the Clemens family residence in Vienna in 1897–1899.[3] True as well, Freud on several occasions indicates his pleasure in the famous American's humor.[4] But there is no evidence at all to indicate the slightest influence in either direction, not even a telling disclaimer of the kind that both directed toward Nietzsche. Twain and Freud worked in complete independence of each other. Yet their shared fascination with the mysteries of the human psyche, and their unflinching witness to the predicament of modern humanity, drew them along often parallel tracks to a range of strikingly similar conclusions.

"The key to the period," according to Ralph Waldo Emerson, was "that the mind had become aware of itself. Men grew reflective and intellectual. There was a new consciousness. . . . The young men were born with knives in their brain, a tendency to introversion, self-dissection, anatomizing of motives."[5] That Freud was such a man is perfectly clear, as Peter Gay observes.[6] Much less obviously, perhaps, Mark Twain must be numbered among those representative figures who turned their attention sharply inward and made of themselves a laboratory of the mind. As a boy in his early teens, Twain proved a willing and able subject for a traveling mesmerist who made a stop in Hannibal in 1850.[7] In 1855, the year before Freud was born, young Twain, then twenty, mined a popular textbook on phrenology for clues to his own volatile personality. He decided, quite astutely, that his was a "burning, flaming, flashing" sanguine temperament.[8] As early as 1862, prompted perhaps by dark memories of childhood sleepwalking and persistent nightmares, Twain reports that he developed "the habit of writing down my dreams of all sorts while they were fresh in my mind, and then studying them and rehearsing them and trying to find out what the source of dreams is, and which of the two or three separate persons inhabiting us is their architect."[9] The interest in split and multiple personality, evident here, is also manifest in his 1869 sketch "The Siamese Twins," where attention falls on the interplay of separate, autonomous, and conflicting impulses in the same person. In 1878, he wrote and then suppressed (for fear of public incredulity) an account of his experiences with "mental telegraphy," in which original ideas are "unconsciously stolen" by one writer from another.[10] Thanks to an early, albeit humorously skeptical, account of a visit to a table-rapping seance, we know that he was also caught up in the fascination with spiritism set in motion in 1847 by the Fox sisters of Hydesville, New York.[11] Years later, his interest assumed a more solemn cast when he and his wife, Livy, consulted mediums in an attempt to communicate with their daughter Susy, who succumbed to meningitis in 1896.[12]

Though never firmly and systematically formulated, Mark Twain's evolving interests in parapsychology coalesced during the last two or three decades of his life, as he attuned himself to waves of European influence more formally embraced in the United States by William James, Morton Prince, G. Stanley Hall, James Jackson Putnam, and others. In 1884, he accepted a membership in the Society for Psychical Research, founded in England by a group headed by F. W. H. Myers.[13] He was also alive to the work of Jean-Martin Charcot, whose dramatic clinical treatment of hysteria at the Sâlpetrière in Paris had gained international acclaim. Desperately seeking psychological help for his daughter Susy in 1894, Twain wrote from New York to his wife in Paris that "the very source, the very *centre* of hypnotism is *Paris*. Dr. Charcot's pupils & disciples are right there & ready to your hand. . . . *Do*, do it, honey. Don't lose a minute."[14]

Several elements feature prominently in the new model of mind that drew Mark Twain into its field of gravitation. At the very center was the unconscious, accessible to hypnotism and fostering kindred notions about dual or multiple personality. The main thrust of what Henri F. Ellenberger describes as this new, "dynamic psychiatry"[15] takes early literary expression in Robert Louis Stevenson's *Strange Case of Dr. Jekyll and Mr. Hyde*, which first appeared in 1886. Twain wrote at length about the story in his notebook in 1897. "Jekyll and Hyde are correct," he judges, "in so far as each has its own separate and distinct nature." But Stevenson erred in making the pair mutually self-aware, Twain believed. "The two persons in a man do not even *know* each other and are not aware of each other's existence," Twain insists. "The French have lately shown (apparently) that that other person is in command during somnambulic sleep," and that "it has a memory of its own and can recall its acts when hypnotized and thrown again into that sleep" (*MTN* 349).[16] We will return in much closer detail to this key text, and to others like it, in due course.

Freud's engagement with the new psychology was of course much more deliberate than Twain's, and the story of his rise to international preeminence as the grand progenitor of psychoanalysis is widely familiar in academic and lay circles. A prodigious student, Freud completed his medical training, with an emphasis on research in physiology, at the University of Vienna in 1881. Four years later, he went to Paris on a traveling fellowship to study with Charcot, an experience that quickened an interest in the treatment of hysteria. Not long after his return to Vienna, he joined his friend Joseph Breuer in the analysis of Anna O, a collaboration that led to the abandonment of hypnosis in favor of free association, dream analysis, the famous "talking cure," and the publication of *Studies in Hysteria* in 1895. Subsequent self-analysis, which fostered pioneering perspectives on the unconscious, repression, the sexual basis and content of dreams, the Oedipal conflict, and the elaborate ways and means of "dream work," culminated in Freud's masterpiece, *The Interpretation of Dreams*, which appeared in 1900. Freud went on in the early decades of the new century to expand and refine his understanding of the intricacies of human psychology, with notable attention to childhood sexuality, unconsciously driven "slips" of the tongue or pen, and a new topographical division of the psyche into three agencies, the id, the ego, and the superego, which replaced the earlier triad featuring the unconscious, the preconscious, and the conscious. He was also increasingly drawn to speculation about the bearing of his scientific theories on the history of civilization, with a special eye to the interplay of the life and death instincts in myth and religion. By the time of his death in 1939, Freud was a global intellectual celebrity and the nonpareil of the expanding psychoanalytic movement.[17]

Though Twain and Freud were temperamentally very different, their lives and intellectual inclinations were analogous in numerous, very striking ways. Both came from large families in the throes of economic hardship; as boys, they were drawn to their mothers and recoiled from their fathers; as adults, both were happily married, caring parents who enjoyed the warmth and material comforts of domesticity; both were hopelessly addicted to cigars. They were as pessimistic about human nature—which they regarded as deeply, perdurably flawed—as they were about the efficacy of political panaceas, including democracy; yet both rebelled against the conservatism of the societies in which they were reared, wrote in defiance of gentility, adopted disenchanted perspectives on childhood innocence, deplored unnatural constraints on human sexuality, supported the emancipation of women, and fiercely opposed anti-Semitism. Both seemed to need a country to hate: Twain loathed the French, Freud the Americans. They were equally skeptical about the possibility of truth in autobiography, yet both were intensely autobiographical in their work.

Twain and Freud agreed that modern humans live in misery. "Life, as we find it," Freud concluded, "is too hard for us; it brings too many pains, disappointments and impossible tasks." He laid the blame for human woe at the door of civilization, with its unnatural insistence on the renunciation of instinct, and argued that we would "be much happier if we gave it up and returned to primitive conditions."[18] Twain emphatically agreed. He observed in creation "an unchanging law" that men and women "should suffer wanton and unnecessary pains and miseries every day of" their lives.[19] Like Freud, he traced human unhappiness to the exigencies of the unnatural demands of civilized morality. Because they failed to recognize the "persecutions of civilization" until too late, he observes in *Following the Equator*, the natives of Tasmania suffered the catastrophic loss of their "wild free life" (*FE* 265).

Twain and Freud deplored the tyranny of guilt in the lives of civilized men and women. Both believed that humans recoil in fear and disgust from the truth about themselves; but they believed as well that the buried truth is resourceful in finding avenues of return, quite in spite of the desire to repress it. They gave emphasis to the formative influence of association in the vagaries of consciousness. They agreed that the unconscious could be a powerful aid to problem solving, that dreams are highly visual, and that sanity and madness are not always easily distinguished. They were instinctive dualists, everywhere attentive to the play of ambivalence. They were resolute determinists. Both were influenced by the ideas of Lamarck and Darwin. Though deeply suspicious of religion, both recognized the power of faith to ease human suffering. They believed that mental illness was susceptible to therapeutic amelioration. Both expressed cautious interest in mental telepathy and the occult. Both became life-weary in their later years, looked with a cold eye on human futurity, and welcomed the end. In much of this—and not least of all in a marked tendency to contradiction—they were of course at one with Nietzsche.

Despite such numerous points of similarity, Twain and Freud were also variously and significantly different. Twain was right to assess himself as volatile. He was given to abrupt, unpredictable swings between a wide range of often fiery moods. Freud, by contrast, was deliberate and balanced in his approach to life. The humorist came to his writing by fits and starts, and valued it in good part because of the wealth it produced. Freud subordinated everything to his work, and worried about money only when there was not enough to meet the comparatively modest needs of his family. Twain regarded women as morally superior to men; Freud took the opposite view. Twain was a master showman who craved the limelight; Freud was a comparatively private person, sober in self-presentation, who aspired to fame as a leader of Mosaic probity and vision. Though they agreed on its often socially subversive thrust, they had very different notions about the dynamics of humor. Twain's determinism was geared to the promise of release from the intolerable burden of guilt, Freud's to a demand for analytical rigor. Twain did not share Freud's dedication to the life of the mind, his disciplined approach to writing, or his faith in science. Twain was intellectually gifted and curious, but as unsystematic in his thinking as he was unpremeditated in his approach to composition. By the terms of his own candid assessment, he was a "jack-leg" novelist who set pen to paper without planning of any kind, and whose plots and characters seemed to develop independently of authorial intention.[20]

Quite in keeping with such erratic habits of mind, Twain's forays into the realm of psychology seldom form fully developed trains of thought and often amount to little more than flashes of artistic intuition. Freud certainly would have understood. A masterfully disciplined architect of ideas, he was at the same time brilliantly attentive to the unconscious origins and significance of apparently accidental or undirected movements of consciousness. There was for Freud no such thing as random utterance, especially among great writers.[21] Shakespeare, he wrote to his friend

Wilhelm Fleiss in 1897, penetrated in *Hamlet* to the very heart of the Oedipal conflict. Yet this was hardly "Shakespeare's conscious intention"; rather, "his unconscious understood the unconscious of his hero."[22] He makes the same claim for the authority of the unconscious in shaping the psychoanalytic insights in Wilhelm Jensen's *Gradiva*. "The author need have known nothing of these rules," Freud is confident, yet "we have not discovered anything in his work that is not already in it." Just so, he would have been quick to recognize the unconscious wellsprings of many of Twain's powerful, albeit spontaneous, insights into the human psyche. "Creative writers are valuable allies," Freud gratefully conceded, "and their evidence is to be prized highly, for they are apt to know a whole host of things between heaven and earth of which our philosophy has not yet let us dream."[23]

Psychoanalysis, Freud rather famously observed, was historically the most recent of three major scientific affronts to naive human self-love. Copernicus banished us from the center of the universe; Darwin shattered the illusion of our privileged position in creation; and psychoanalysis showed us that the ego "is not even master in its own house, but must content itself with scanty information of what is going on unconsciously in its mind."[24] Frank J. Sulloway observes that Freud was first exposed to the existence and potent authority of the unconscious in 1885 during his fellowship in Paris. Charcot's famous clinical presentations, with their dramatic use of hypnotism, revealed to the young Viennese physician "that multiple states of consciousness could simultaneously coexist in one and the same individual without either state apparently having knowledge of the other."[25] As we have seen, Twain drew deeply from the same source. Indeed, in his commentary linking Stevenson's *Dr. Jekyll and Mr. Hyde* with Charcot's demonstrations of multiple, independent personalities, Twain recalls that his 1876 essay "The Facts Concerning the Recent Carnival of Crime in Connecticut" was "an attempt to account for our seeming *duality*—the presence in us of another *person*; not a slave of ours, but free and independent, and with a character distinctly its own." As we shall see in due course, it was also vitally significant that Twain identified "that other person" in himself with his conscience, "a malignant dwarf," very much his "own master," whose sole purpose is to inflict guilt (*MTN* 348).

Clearly, then, Twain was at one with Freud on the reality and importance of the unconscious, on the existence in the same individual of multiple, autonomous states of consciousness, and on the uses of hypnosis. They agreed as well that the unconscious transcends time and mortality, and operates completely without restraint. In his essay "Negation," Freud declares that "in analysis we never discover a 'no' in the unconscious."[26] He elaborates in "The Unconscious" that "the processes of the system *Ucs.* are *timeless*; i.e. they are not ordered temporally, are not altered by the passage of time; they have no reference to time at all."[27] Nor does the unconscious "believe in its own death," he notes in "Thoughts for the Times on War and Death"; "it behaves as if it were immortal."[28] Decades earlier, Twain came to virtually identical conclusions. In "My Platonic Sweetheart," a dream narrative composed in the late 1890s, he draws back from his story to describe "the artist in us who constructs our dreams," an unconscious creative force "many hundreds of times the superior of the poor thing in us who architects our waking thoughts." He goes on to recall both his earlier, "crude attempt to work out the duality idea" in "The Recent Carnival of Crime," and his efforts in subsequent reflections on Robert Louis Stevenson's Jekyll and Hyde and "the French experiments in hypnosis." Expanding on this background, he divides the individual into three "persons": the waking self; an entirely independent "somnambulist partner" whose "commonplace" experiences "can be reproduced by hypnotism"; and the vastly superior "dream-self," or "dream-artist," who transports the dreamer to experiences of limitless variety and indescribable vividness and intensity. In this fabulous realm, everything is possible, time and space have no meaning, and the world is "immortal and indestructible."[29]

Twain set out a variant on the same tripartite conception of the self in *No. 44, The Mysterious Stranger*—the final version of the series of fragments known collectively as *The Mysterious Stranger*—which he worked on during the last years of his life. The role of the dream-self in *No. 44* is taken by Emil Schwarz, the embodiment of what Susan Gillman has rightly described as "the creative unconscious" of the story's narrator, August Feldner.[30] August readily admits that Emil is his superior. "My imagination, compared with his splendid dream-equipment, was as a lightning bug to the lightning. . . . In passion, feeling, emotion, sensation—whether of pain or pleasure—I was phosphorous, he was fire. In a word he had all the intensities one suffers or enjoys in a dream!" As a "spirit of the air," what Emil feels most intensely of all is the torment of his embodiment in mortal flesh. Those who inhabit "the august Empire of Dreams," he explains to August, "have no home, no prison, the universe is our province; we do not know time, we do not know space—we live, and love, and labor, and enjoy, fifty years in an hour, while you are sleeping. . . . We circumnavigate your little globe while you wink" (*MS* 344, 370).[31] Freud's definition of a dream—"a (disguised) fulfillment of a (suppressed or repressed) wish"[32]—is of course well known. A dream is the expression of unconscious impulses that reach consciousness only at the price of distortion wrought by the "dream work" in order to elude censorship. The meaning of the dream, its "latent content," is clarified in the course of the analysis of its "manifest content," as it is recalled by the dreamer. Twain's writing also clearly suggests that dreams disclose, vividly if often obscurely, our deepest desires. "My Platonic Sweetheart" is the narrative of a recurrent dream of highly "spiritualized" romantic love for which he had an apparent longing. It contrasts sharply with another erotic dream, this one recorded in an 1897 notebook entry, in which he recounts a decidedly sexual encounter with a "negro wench." We will analyze these dreams in due course, giving attention to their expression of repressed desires inadmissible in uncensored form to the conscious light of day.

As John S. Tuckey demonstrated some years ago, it is hardly possible to separate Twain's emergent dream "theory" from the feelings of loss and anguished guilt that overtook him in the later years of his life.[33] There was a humiliating plunge into bankruptcy in 1894, then the death of his favorite daughter, Susy, two years later. The writer retreated from the anguish of these and other setbacks into the thought that life must be a nightmare from which he would surely awaken; or, alternatively, that a seeming dream of disaster was in fact an intolerable reality from which there was no relief. This uncertain boundary between dream and waking experience is centrally at play in the late dream writings—"Which Was the Dream?" "The Great Dark," "Which Was It?" and "Three Thousand Years among the Microbes" notable among them—in which characters cling to the hope that they may wind up on the right side of the ambiguous divide. Twain took a further step along these lines just after the death of his wife, Livy, in 1904. In response to an inquiry from his old friend Joseph Twichell about his views on "life and the world—the past and the future," he wrote,

> (A *part* of each day—or night) as they have been looking to me the past 7 years: as being NON-EXISTENT. That is, that there is *nothing*. That there is no God and no universe; that there is only empty space, and in it a lost and homeless and wandering and companionless and indestructible *Thought*. And that I am that thought. And God, and the Universe, and Time, and Life, and Death, and Joy and Sorrow and Pain only a grotesque and brutal *dream*, evolved from the frantic imagination of that insane Thought.[34]

It is the clear implication of Twain's desperate recoil from waking reality into an oneiric realm of unrestrained solipsism that the world is as boundless as the unconscious imagination that dreams it into existence. Borrowing directly from his letter to Twichell, he makes this crystal clear in No. 44's final advice to the astonished August Feldner: You are and will forever "remain a *Thought*," he declares, "the only existent Thought, and by your nature inextinguishable, indestructible." It follows that you are at liberty to shape and inhabit the reality of your deepest longings. Therefore, "dream other dreams, and better!" (*MS* 404).

Like the Freudian unconscious, then, Twain's creative dream-self operates with complete freedom from restraints of all kinds, including the limits of space, time, and intimations of mortality, and it is the voice of the deepest of human wishes. But unrestraint is fraught with the danger that accompanies the lack of all moral compunction. "Our unconscious will murder even for trifles,"[35] Freud acknowledged. Quite aptly, Peter Gay likens the Freudian unconscious to "a maximum-security prison holding antisocial inmates . . . barely kept under control and forever attempting to escape."[36] By a different route, Twain came to a similar view. The figure of Satan in the first version of *The Mysterious Stranger* is an embodiment of the unconscious dream life of Philip Traum, who narrates the story. Philip recoils in horror as his fascinating companion massacres hundreds of innocent people. "It is no matter," Satan comments blithely, "we can make more" (*MS* 52). Freedom from the contemptible Moral Sense, and hence from guilt, spells release to murderous impulses at the dark heart of human nature. After Twain finally kills his conscience in "The Facts Concerning the Recent Carnival of Crime in Connecticut," he promptly indulges himself in a season of gratifying murder and mayhem. "Bliss, unalloyed bliss," he exults. "Nothing in all the world could persuade me to have a conscience again."[37]

Mark Twain's imagined murder of his conscience humorously enacts what Freud defined as repression. "The essence of repression," he explains, "lies simply in turning something away, and keeping it at a distance, from the conscious." He goes on to add that "the motive and purpose of repression [is] nothing else than the avoidance of unpleasure" (*SE* 14:147)—the unpleasure, in "The Recent Carnival of Crime," of having to bear the guilt for indulging instinctual aggression. The same distancing from consciousness is dramatized in *The Adventures of Tom Sawyer*, when the young hero closes his mind to the dangerous knowledge that it was Injun Joe, and not Muff Potter, who murdered Dr. Robinson in the town graveyard. Twain was himself quite prone to repression, especially—as Terrell Dempsey has recently demonstrated—when it came to the management of memories of his childhood experiences of slavery.[38] Retreat from painful moral implication along these lines shapes the action of *Adventures of Huckleberry Finn*. This is most conspicuously the case, perhaps, when Huck, having played a cruel and dangerous practical joke involving snakes on his friend, the escaped slave, Jim, decides to conceal the evidence of what he has done. "I warn't going to let Jim find out it was all my fault," he says, "not if I could help it" (*HF* 65). But in concealing the damaging truth from his friend, Huck attempts—as the subsequent narrative makes clear—to conceal it from himself as well.

Mark Twain was unable to contain what he remembered about the old slave times in Hannibal, just as Huck is unable to strike the memory of the snake skins completely from his consciousness. They both exhibit what Freud describes—in *Moses and Monotheism*, for example—as the "return of the repressed," when materials banished to the unconscious resurface in distorted or compromised form.[39] Thus Twain's writing is replete with oblique or substantially modified or distorted versions of his dark memories of slavery; and Huck is on several occasions reminded of the snake skins, though always in ways that reduce their full moral weight. As for Tom, he is finally unable to contain what he has repressed about the murder; quite characteristically, however, he contrives to reveal the life-saving truth in a self-aggrandizing spectacle that successfully distracts attention from the fact of its prolonged concealment.

The unsummoned return of the repressed is the surest evidence that humans have very limited control over their secrets from themselves and others. Freud confidently observes that "he who has eyes to see and ears to hear becomes convinced that mortals can keep no secret. If their lips are silent, they gossip with their fingertips; betrayal forces its way through every pore."[40] In the self-analysis recorded in *The Interpretation of Dreams*, and in the analysis of his patients in the case histories, Freud unpacks the concealed psychological significance of free associations, play and fantasy, screen memories, psychosomatic symptoms, and experiences of the uncanny. In a more popular vein, *The Psychopathology of Everyday Life* is a narrative of detection in which apparently meaningless slips are scrutinized for inadvertent disclosures of unconscious motives. To one skilled in their interpretation, Freud demonstrates, the interior lives of human beings are an open book.

Like Freud, Twain was his own best laboratory on the futility of secrecy. His ambivalent feelings about his brother, Henry, for example, are baldly manifest in the textbook screen memory of his younger sibling "walking into a fire outdoors when he was a week old" (*AMT* 3). Twain seems to have missed the significance of this telling slip, but he was nonetheless sharply attentive to the inadvertent self-revelations broadcast elsewhere in his writing. "Autobiography," he found while writing his own, "is the truest of all books; for while it inevitably consists mainly of extinctions of the truth, shirkings of the truth, partial revealments of the truth, with hardly an instance of plain straight truth, the remorseless truth *is* there, between the lines, where the author cat is raking dust upon it which hides from the disinterested spectator neither it nor its smell . . . the result being that the reader knows the author in spite of his wily diligences."[41]

Huck is similarly knowing about unwitting self-betrayals. He decides against telling Mary Jane about the nefarious schemes of the king and the duke for fear that "her face would give them a hint, sure" (*HF* 225–26).[42] Despite such shrewdness, however, Huck's failure to control his own body language derails his attempt to convince the discerning but kindly Judith Loftus that he is a girl (*HF* 68–75). Tom Sawyer is equally transparent when his anxious secret about the murder takes what Freud would have recognized as hysterical expression in the onset of a psychosomatic illness. "It was a chronic misery," the boy complains. "It was a very cancer for permanency and pain. Then came the measles" (*TS* 178–79).

As for the uncanny—a frightening conjunction, according to Freud, of what is at once familiar and forgotten or repressed[43]—it is a psychological phenomenon inextricably bound up in Twain's writing with his lifelong interest in doubling and twinning. When Italian Siamese twins turn up in *Pudd'nhead Wilson and Those Extraordinary Twins*, for example, the citizens of the slaveholding town of St. Petersburg are "conscious of nothing but that prodigy, that uncanny apparition . . . that weird strange thing that was so soft spoken and so gentle of manner, and yet had shaken them up like an earthquake with the shock of its grewsome aspect" (*PW* 131). The conspicuous excess of this reaction has its source in repressed intimations that the boundary separating the races in southern society is "a fiction of law and custom," an artificial sundering of people actually akin to one another (*PW* 9).[44]

It is the crystal-clear implication of theories foregrounding repression and the unconscious that human beings are strongly inclined to varieties of self-deception. "Lying is universal," Twain insisted; "we *all* do it."[45] Freud agreed. John Forrester argues persuasively that psychoanalysis is "founded on the expectation that the subject will, inevitably, being human, lie." Dreams are not true or false; they arise out of the unconscious, a "psychic reality" in which the distinction between truth and fiction has no relevance. Thus Freud suspended moral condemnation of lying and deception, especially in the analytic setting, where—as Forrester puts it—he subordinated "the discourse of blame to the discourse of discovery."[46] Twain made gestures toward a similar moral neutrality. Because lying is universally the expression of an immutable law of human nature, he argued, it is inculpable.[47] But even as he strained to forgive, Twain condemned liars, not least of all because he numbered himself first among them.

Both writers recognized and valued the narrative yield of free association. Guided by his "fundamental rule" in psychoanalytic treatment, Freud asked his patients to say whatever came to mind, selecting or omitting nothing, however unpleasant or seemingly irrelevant. The process was understood to be entirely spontaneous, without regard to truth or falsehood.[48] Twain fell into a virtually identical approach to composition, whether in fiction or nonfiction. "I never deliberately sat down and 'created' a character in my life," he wrote in 1907. "In fact, every book I ever wrote just wrote itself."[49] This included his autobiography, to which he applied what he called "the methodless method" of the human mind. "I . . . talk about the matter which for the moment interests me, and cast it aside and talk about something else the moment its interest for me is exhausted." In thus following the path of least resistance, he was conforming to "the law of *narrative*, which *has no law*."[50] No apparent law, that is; for Twain shared Freud's assumption, based on copious experience, that the random-seeming flood of associations would, once interpreted, yield clear if often unanticipated meanings.

Freud viewed universal deceit and self-deception as inevitable corollaries of civilization. "It is impossible," he asserts, "to overlook the extent to which civilization is built up upon a renunciation of instinct, how much it presupposes precisely the non-satisfaction (by suppression, repression or some other means?) of powerful instincts."[51] Such "cultural frustration" produces compromise formations in which we simultaneously bend to irresistible gratifications and to the prohibitions against them. "Self-deception and hypocrisy," maintains Peter Gay, "which substitute good reasons for real reasons, are the conscious companions of repression, denying passionate needs for the sake of family concord, social harmony, or sheer respectability."[52]

Huck Finn, who is perfectly "free and satisfied" with his irregular ways, struggles to avoid such binds. But things go from bad to worse when the widow Douglas and Miss Watson take him in and commence to "civilizing" him. The widow "put me in them new clothes again," he complains, "and I couldn't do nothing but sweat and sweat, and feel all cramped up" (*HF* 2). Things are much better out on the wide Mississippi with Jim. "Other places do seem so cramped up and smothery," Huck observes, "but a raft don't. You feel mighty free and easy and comfortable on a raft" (*HF* 155). Twain felt the same way. Like Freud, he blamed suffocating, contradictory civilized morality for the repression, the self-deception, and the hypocrisy. "There is a Moral Sense," he wrote, "and there is an Immoral Sense. History shows us that the Moral Sense enables us to perceive morality and how it avoid it, and that the Immoral Sense enables us to perceive immorality and how to enjoy it" (*FE* 161).

The catalog of parallels between the thought of Freud and Twain—parallels striking not least of all because of their independence—might be extended at some length. Nor can one too much emphasize the similarities in their thinking on the authority of the unconscious, the significance of dreams, the developmental importance of childhood, the psychodynamics of art, the corrosive influence of religion, and the deep divisions in the modern psyche. Had the opportunity arisen to share their views on these and other, cognate matters, they would have found much to agree upon, and no little pleasure, I suspect, in their differences of approach, expression, and personality. Given time, they might have chanced as well upon broader if perhaps less looked-for convergences in their interests and ideas: on the pleasure principle, for example; or guilt; or the present and future condition of civilized humanity. These are the topics that will occupy us for the duration.

Freud and Twain enjoyed their families, derived great satisfaction from their work, and took their pleasures with gusto. But neither of them truly loved life; in fact, for both the sum of suffering in human experience vastly outweighed the sum of joy. And though both knew something of physical pain, it was the weight of mental anguish that most impressed them. Worse yet, there was no cure for the living. Work, love, religion, therapeutic interventions—these might help a little along the way, but their benefits were fleeting and largely illusory. The only durable stay against suffering, they agreed, was release from the torment of consciousness into sleep, oblivion, death itself.

How ironic, then, that Freud's views on the subject should have their foundation in what he called "the pleasure principle." He did not share the romantic notion, identified most closely perhaps with Keats, Pater, and Emma Bovary, that more is better when it comes to emotional intensity. He wrote, quite to the contrary, that "unpleasurable feelings are connected with an increase and pleasurable feelings with a decrease of stimulus."[53] In the service of this principle, our interior lives are regulated by a reflex inclination to avoid or to release mental tension. Thus in sexual experience—the model for the pleasure/unpleasure nexus—ultimate satisfaction is achieved not in "highly intensified excitation," but in "its final elimination in the pleasure of discharge."[54] As Kaja Silverman points out, in defining pleasure as "the zero degree of tension," Freud sets our deepest human longings on course toward "a state of relaxation much more intimately connected with death than with life."[55]

Though it is much less theoretical in its formulation, there is in Mark Twain's writing a virtually identical tendency to associate unpleasure with increased stimulation and pleasure with its progressive reduction toward the ultimate goal of blissfully complete oblivion. Consciousness for Twain, as for Freud, is the principal locus of human suffering. It is a lightly armed outpost, placid in isolation, but vulnerable at all times to sudden, devastating assaults, and to prolonged, wasting occupations, taking their rise from various quarters, but principally from the lawless regions of the unconscious. We crave repose, Freud believed, but it is our lot to be engaged in ceaseless psychic warfare against encroachments of "unpleasurable tension."[56] Twain observed, nearly two decades earlier: "We are so made that we will pay *anything* for . . . contentment—even another man's life. . . . [We] *must* have rest and peace—it is the law of our nature."[57]

It is of course very striking that two writers of such different temperaments coming from such contrasting backgrounds and intellectual environments should have arrived independently at this equally striking conception of human mental experience— and most centrally, of consciousness—as fragile, embattled, struggling desperately and quite in vain for a serenity not to be had on this side of the grave. Viewed in light of its central, widely ramifying significance in the larger frame of each writer's work, this shared perspective is all the more remarkable. Freud expressed "no hesitation in assuming that the course taken by mental events"— that is to say, the complex totality of human functioning in thought, feeling, and eventual action—"is automatically regulated by the pleasure principle."[58] Twain was similarly sensitized to the relentless agitation of unsettling intrusions into consciousness. His first major book, *The Innocents Abroad*, affords us a window on mental turmoil so persistent and intense as to engender a longing for oblivion—for "nothing less," in Roger B. Salomon's terms, "than severance of the direct relationship between the mind and the world."[59] Most of his later work, and virtually all of his fiction, gives prominence to characters—Tom Sawyer, Huckleberry Finn, Hank Morgan, Tom Driscoll, and Theodor Fischer prominent among them—so tormented by dark, intense, unsummoned thoughts and feelings that they fall prey to a desire for death.

Freud and Twain agree that our fundamental goal in mental experience is the avoidance of the pain that accompanies increases of stimulation, most especially mental stimulation arising without warning from the unconscious. We are not hedonists bent on ever more pleasure; rather, pleasure for us is defined negatively as the diminished influence of its dread opposite. We seek relief from stress in repose. But while they agreed that heightened excitation is the enemy, they took different views of its source and specific nature. For Freud, unpleasure is traceable to the demand for satisfaction of repressed and therefore unconscious infantile wishes, predominantly sexual in nature, that make their way, modified by the dream work to avoid censorship, into our dreams, jokes, parapraxes, and neuroses.[60] Their sexuality, broadly conceived, is thus primarily responsible for the unpleasurable extremes of stimulation from which humans recoil.[61]

The role that sex plays in Freud's characterization of the pleasure principle is taken in Twain's by guilt. It is thus guilt, as we began to see in the Introduction, that links him firmly to both Freud and Nietzsche, who focuses on the significance of guilt in *The Genealogy of Morals.* Here we reexamine some of the same examples in order to stress both the similarities and the differences between the sages and Twain, the jester, on this key topic. "Man hides himself from himself during most hours of the day," observes the interlocutor in *What Is Man?* But the self-deception gives way to the truth "when he wakes out of sleep, deep in the night. You know the bitterness of that hour; we all know it. The black thoughts come flocking through our brain, they show us our naked soul, our true soul, and we perceive and confess that we are despicable."[62] The balm of sleep is thus shattered by ungovernable incursions of self-loathing into consciousness. Human torment takes many forms, but in Twain's case it came most frequently and most painfully as guilt. "Remorse was always Samuel Clemens's surest punishment," observes his first biographer, Albert Bigelow Paine; "to his last days on earth he never outgrew its pangs."[63] And as we recall, Twain's conscience exults in "The Facts Concerning the Recent Carnival of Crime in Connecticut," "It is my *business*—and my joy—to make you repent of *every*thing you do" (*CTSSE* 1:654).

Like both Nietzsche and Freud, Twain is among those moderns who find conscience deeply problematic—even more so than the European sages, as we now see clearly, he was at war with it. For while there is some ambiguity in Freud's treatment of the sources of unpleasure, there is none in Twain's. "Good friends, good books and a sleepy conscience," he observes in his notebook: "this is the ideal life" (MTN 347). As pointed out previously, Twain quarrels bitterly with his embodied conscience in "The Recent Carnival of Crime"; then he kills him. The immediate result: he is restored to the blissful indulgence of his instincts. When it comes to guilt, Huck Finn is similarly decisive: "If I had a yaller dog that didn't know no more than a person's conscience," he reflects, "I would pison him" (*HF* 290). Whether a source of morbid inhibition and "slave morality," as in Nietzsche, or neurotic symptoms, as in Freud, the dirty dog deserves to die.

More routinely, the novelist and his most famous character seek relief from moral stress by taking to the water. As we have seen, Huck experiences his greatest comfort and satisfaction when he is out on the Mississippi with Jim. The "soft and peaceful beauty" of summertime in Germany is best appreciated, Twain notes in *A Tramp Abroad*, when one travels at a leisurely pace down a wide river. "The motion of a raft is the needful motion; it is gentle, and gliding, and smooth, and noiseless; it calms down all feverish activities, it soothes to sleep all nervous hurry and impatience; under its restful influence all the troubles and vexations and sorrows that harass the mind vanish away, and existence becomes a dream, a charm, a deep and tranquil ecstasy."[64] Ten days of rafting down the Rhone in 1891, he wrote to his close friend Joseph Twichell, left his "conscience in a state of coma, and lazy comfort, and solid happiness. In fact there's *nothing* that's so lovely."[65] But Twain's guilt-driven deployment of the pleasure principle is best illustrated in a passage from the manuscript of *The Innocents Adrift*, which Albert Bigelow Paine abridged for posthumous publication in *Europe and Elsewhere*. "To glide down the stream in an open boat, moved by the current only," and thereby to experience the "strange absence of the sense of sin, and the stranger absence of the desire to commit it"[66]—such freedom from moral anxiety was the height of attainable mortal bliss.

Determinism, it is clear, was preeminent among Twain's strategies for reducing the unpleasure of guilt. "Why do you reproach yourself?" No. 44 obligingly inquires when August Feldner acknowledges his grave moral failings. "You did not make yourself; how then are you to blame?" (*MS* 250). Twain sought similar consolation in the easeful influence of memory, and in the softened perspectives produced by the retreat from discord across expanded stretches of space and time.[67] But the exploration of the pleasure principle immanent in his work is most like Freud's when he turns his attention to sleep and death. Freud describes sleep as "a reactivation of intrauterine existence, fulfilling as it does the conditions of repose, warmth and exclusion of stimulus; indeed, in sleep many people resume the foetal posture. The psychical state of a sleeping person is characterized by an almost complete withdrawal from the surrounding world and a cessation of all interest in it."[68] He works a close variation on the same theme in *Introductory Lectures on Psychoanalysis*, emphasizing that "I put myself to sleep by withdrawing from the external world and keeping its stimuli away from me."[69] Twain takes the identical line, insisting that the goal of sleep is to banish all thought of the world and thereby to reduce stimulation to a pleasurable minimum. After an especially hectic day of travel, sleep descends in *The Innocents Abroad* as "a great calm of forgetfulness and peace."[70] Just so, its balm of "peace—stillness deep and solemn" (*FE* 353) is gratefully embraced in circumstances of heightened moral stress in *Following the Equator*. Huck finds himself in similar circumstances on the wreck of the *Walter Scott*; when he is finally reunited with Jim at nightfall, he reports that "they turned in and slept like dead people" (*HF* 92). In the same way, No. 44's concluding injunction to "dream other dreams, and better" answers August Feldner's desperate need to break free from the moral absurdity of the world as he finds it.

But of course there is no permanent escape for the living into "conditions of repose, warmth and exclusion of stimulus." It is one thing to enjoin better dreams (as in some sense and various ways Nietzsche, Freud, and Marx all did), but quite another— as Twain well knew, and as *The Mysterious Stranger* shows—to succeed in having them. Trips on the water terminate on land; good memories are hardly proof against bad; sleep is temporary, and subject to unpleasurable disruptions. The strain of stress, and most especially the incubus of guilt, may be temporarily assuaged, but never outrun for long. Except in death. "Annihilation has no terrors for me," Twain declares in his autobiography. "I have already tried it before I was born—a hundred million years—and I have suffered more in an hour, in this life, than I remember to have suffered in the whole hundred million years put together. There was a peace, a serenity, an absence of all sense of responsibility, an absence of worry, an absence of care, grief, perplexity; and the presence of a deep content and unbroken satisfaction in that hundred million years of holiday which I look back upon with a tender longing and with a grateful desire to resume, when the opportunity comes" (*AMT* 249).

The wish to die is never far from the mind of poor, haunted Huck Finn. He expresses in fictional form a longing for release that his maker voiced with ever-greater urgency and frequency in his later years: "Adam, man's benefactor—he gave him all he has ever received that was worth having—Death" (MTN 368). "The suicide seems to me the only sane person" (MTN 381). "Race suicide . . . the only valuable human disease I've struck in the cornucopia yet."[71] "Why is it that we rejoice at birth and grieve at a funeral? It is because we are not the person involved" (*PW* 44). Death, "that dear and sweet and kindly one, that steeps in dreamless and enduring sleep the pains that persecute the body, and the shames and griefs that eat the mind and heart. Bring it! I am weary, I would rest."[72] Finally, to put the seal on this litany to death, here is an especially powerful passage from "Letters from the Earth":

Life was not a valuable gift, but death was. Life was a feverish dream made up of joys embittered by sorrows, pleasure poisoned by pain; a dream that was a nightmare-confusion of spasmodic and fleeting delights, ecstasies, exultations, happinesses, interspersed with long-drawn miseries, griefs, perils, horrors, disappointments, defeats, humiliations and despairs—the heaviest curse devisable by divine ingenuity; but death was sweet, death was gentle, death was kind, death healed the bruised spirit and the broken heart, and gave them rest and forgetfulness; death was man's best friend, his only friend; when man could endure life no longer, death came, and set him free.[73]

Freud did not long for death with anything like Twain's fervor, but he greeted it voluntarily when his life's pain grew intolerable. And he would have understood the warmth of Twain's response to the allure of the end. Freud was quite sure, after all, "that the intention that man should be 'happy' is not included in the plan of 'Creation.'"[74] Yet the strong tilt toward death built into his thought did not fully emerge until 1920, when Freud announced in *Beyond the Pleasure Principle* "that there really does exist in the mind a compulsion to repeat which overrides the pleasure principle." He found evidence for this novel behavior in children's games, in the dreams of neurotic patients, and in the need felt by veterans to relive their traumatic wartime experiences. In the latter instances, "the pleasure principle is for the moment put out of action" and the mental apparatus is "flooded with large amounts of stimulus," all of it painful.[75] Such suffering, Freud argues, is in the service of instinctual impulses that operate independently of the pleasure principle, and that seek to restore the organism to an earlier inorganic state. Life naturally tends, in other words, toward its own dissolution. Freud then positions this elemental death drive in direct opposition to the sexual drive, which is composed of the procreative instincts that strive to foster and prolong existence. Thus life also tends naturally toward its own perpetuation. In the upshot, we have the familiar—and perfectly radical—distinction between Eros and Thanatos.

Had Mark Twain lived long enough to own and read *Beyond the Pleasure Principle*, he would have been struck by a satisfying shock of recognition. There was sanction for his own experience in Freud's declaration that "the dominating tendency of mental life . . . is the effort to reduce, to keep constant or to remove internal tension due to stimuli . . . a tendency which finds expression in the pleasure principle." And his rapidly gathering interest would have peaked at the point of Freud's acknowledgment that this tendency—which he identifies as the "Nirvana principle"—"is one of our strongest reasons for believing in the existence of death instincts." Here was the clearest confirmation that Twain was not alone in his compulsion to revisit memories of intense unpleasure, and that his recurrent remorse conformed to a pattern of vexed overstimulation for which death was the natural, and the only, cure. From the midst of the argument, there can be no doubt that he would have paused over, and then underlined, Freud's declaration that "the aim of all life is death."[76] The words are startling, of course. But they are no more startling than the fact that America's favorite humorist should have arrived independently at a closely analogous perspective. Twain agreed with Freud that death must be a central element in any serious interpretation of human experience. Drawing on bitter personal history, he agreed as well that all life tends toward extinction, and that this is so because human beings retreat instinctively from fretful stimulation toward the lure of a repose verging on oblivion.

Freud's thought, according to Adam Phillips, is grounded in assumptions about what "people cannot bear to remember, experience, or know. These essential terrors define what it is to be human; or what, in order to be human, one feels obliged to exclude. Psychoanalytic theory is a theory of the unbearable, of what one prefers not to know."[77] The principal psychological mechanism for excluding the unbearable is of course repression, "the cornerstone," Freud insisted, "on which the whole structure of psychoanalysis rests."[78] Freud went on to explain that "the essence of repression lies simply in turning something away, and keeping it at a distance, from the conscious."[79] The things turned away and kept at a distance, he believed, were almost invariably traceable to origins in unconscious sexual instincts. What we fear and hide from in ourselves, then, is our perverse, refractory sexuality.

Mark Twain told the same basic story, but with guilt in place of sex in the leading role. To be sure, the humorist's version was even more closely personal than Freud's. Years after her father's death, Clara Clemens paused to comment on the perversity of his subjection to guilt: "Self-condemnation was the natural turn for his mind to take, yet often he accused himself of having inflicted pain or trouble when the true cause was far removed from himself."[80] Twain's autobiography is replete with painful memories of real and imagined childhood transgressions. "I took all the tragedies to myself," he recalls, "and tallied them off in turn as they happened, saying to myself in each case, with a sigh, 'Another one gone—and on my account; this ought to bring me to repentance; the patience of God will not always endure.'" Nor had the habituation to guilt eased at all in his adult life. "In my age, as in my youth," he concedes wearily, "night brings me many a deep remorse. I realize that from the cradle up I have been like the rest of the race—never quite sane in the night" (*AMT* 42–43).

We have touched more than once on Twain's memorable representation of his mortal struggle with guilt in "The Facts Concerning the Recent Carnival of Crime in Connecticut." The view of his own conscience taken there—as an irrational, remorseless agent of torment—is the basic model from which the writer drew in his many literary treatments of "the rest of the race." This is to say that Twain's characters fear and repress guilt in much the same way that Freud's patients fear and repress the sexual instincts. Illustrative examples abound. As we have seen, Tom Sawyer's desperate attempt to repress his guilty knowledge about the murder brings on a hysterical case of the measles. Nor is the boy alone in his suffering. When she learns about the tragedy, his aunt Polly inadvertently betrays her repressed sense of complicity in Dr. Robinson's death. "Sho!" she exclaims. "It's that dreadful murder. I dream about it most every night myself. Sometimes I dream it's me that done it" (*TS* 105). And in concealing the snake skins in the bushes, Huck Finn tries to elude the guilt that hangs over him because of his cruel practical joke on Jim. *Pudd'nhead Wilson* is the portrait of a community that has deeply repressed the unbearable truth about the cruelty and moral cowardice of its main social institution, race-slavery. "The Man That Corrupted Hadleyburg" is the portrait of a community that has deeply repressed

the unbearable truth about its own dishonesty. Such people perfectly exemplify the leading principle of Twain's philosophical
treatise, *What Is Man?*—that human beings are motivated first
and foremost to secure the peace of mind that comes with moral
self-approval—and link Twain to Nietzsche, as we have argued.
But they win their way to the goal of equanimity not by sticking
to the path of commonsense virtue nor by any Nietzschean "self-
overcoming"—and we stress here, *much less* by any lucid analysis
of self, as in Freud—but with the aid of the Moral Sense, which, as
we have seen, enables them to eclipse from consciousness the accusing reality of their departures from the straight and narrow.[81]

Like Freud, then, Twain was centrally preoccupied with the unbearable things that human beings prefer not to know, and with
the mechanisms of their repression. The distinction between the
roles of sex and guilt in their perspectives is well founded, I believe, though in some respects the difference may be more apparent than real. Consider that Freud's early insistence on the
near absolute primacy of repressed sexual motives conflicts utterly with what he so brilliantly demonstrates in his first venture
into dream analysis. The detailed treatment of his famous Irma
dream of July 23–24, 1895, has nothing apparently to do with sex,
and focuses instead on his impulse to suppress unconscious guilt
feelings about challenges to his sense of professional competence.
The dream, he concludes, "represented a particular state of affairs
as I should have wished it to be," and thus afforded Freud his first
powerful confirmation of the idea that "a dream is a (disguised)
fulfilment of a (suppressed or repressed) wish."[82]

How striking it is that guilt figures centrally in Freud's inaugural dream analysis, yet plays no part at all in his broader understanding of his subject. "The more one is concerned with the
solution of dreams," he observes in his classic study, "the more one
is driven to recognize that the majority of the dreams of adults
deal with sexual material and give expression to erotic wishes."[83]
Sex and sexually related topics take up two columns in the index
of *The Interpretation of Dreams*; guilt is not listed.[84] But if the conspicuous guilt in the Irma dream is notably without subsequent
theoretical impact, what of the apparent absence from the dream

of the sexual motive so conspicuous in the book's larger scheme? I repeat the word *apparent* because there is in Freud's analysis the hint of a sexual motive that is no sooner broached than summarily brushed aside. Midway in the dream, Freud's "friend" Leopold examines Irma "through her bodice" and makes a diagnostic observation about the skin on her left shoulder. "I noticed this, just as he did," Freud remarks, "in spite of her dress." In his subsequent analysis, Freud deflects attention away from this suggestive passage by insisting that "the wording of the dream was most ambiguous: '*I noticed this, just as he did* . . .' I noticed it in my own body, that is." Quite improbably, then, Freud asks us to believe that the skin problem he refers to in the dream is his, not Irma's. He goes on to dismiss the words "in spite of her dress" as a mere "interpolation," adding that he once knew of a "celebrated physician" who examined his female patients through their clothes. "Further than this," he concludes, "I could not see. Frankly, I had no desire to penetrate more deeply at this point."[85]

The sexually inflected ambiguities here are quite extraordinary. Is it that he can see no further than this into the significance of these provocative details? Or, rather, is it Irma's gown that obstructs his interested gaze? Evidently startled by the awkward intimation of a sexual motive, Freud makes matters worse by disavowing a "desire to penetrate," which inadvertently betrays an unconscious wish to do just that. Irma, it seems irresistibly clear, is the object of her analyst's repressed sexual desires. Are we thus witness in the text's startling revelations to the original Freudian slip? Or, more likely, must we suppose that Freud was being entirely consistent in detecting an unconscious sexual motive in his dream, but that for obvious reasons of professional discretion (painfully at issue in the dream itself, after all), he elected to disclose that motive in the most ambiguous way possible? I am inclined to take the latter view, that the slip was intentional. But either way, it seems clear that his dream about the disguised fulfillment of a repressed wish for moral vindication in matters of professional competence is also a dream in which professionally inappropriate sexual desires are obliquely manifest.[86]

Turning now to Mark Twain, we will find a similar entanglement of *sex and guilt* where we were initially disposed to find
guilt alone. As we have seen, guilt takes as high a profile in Twain's
work as sex does in Freud's. "His moods of remorse seemed to
overwhelm him at times," reports Albert Bigelow Paine. "He
spoke of [his brother] Henry's death and little [son] Langdon's
and charged himself with both. He declared that for years he
had filled Mrs. Clemens's life with privations, that the sorrow
of Susy's death had hastened her own. How darkly he painted
it! One saw the jester, who for forty years had been making the
world laugh, performing always before a background of tragedy."[87] These and other transgressions—some real, some imagined, all exaggerated—had a part to play in virtually all of Twain's
writing, but most especially in the major fiction, where he was
freest with the dark truth because he was least aware that he was
disclosing it.[88] Twain's surrender to unconscious impulses in his
writing contrasts quite sharply, of course, with Freud's judicious
self-awareness.

Nothing in his past weighed more heavily on Mark Twain's
conscience than his childhood involvement in race-slavery. "No
man more perfectly sensed, and more entirely abhorred, slavery," wrote his good friend William Dean Howells. "He held himself responsible for the wrong which the white race had done the
black race in slavery, and he explained, in paying the way of a negro student through Yale, that he was doing it as part of the repa-
ration due from every white man to every black man."[89] But good
deeds were accompanied by increasingly troubled thoughts.
"Whenever a colored man commits an unright action," Twain
wrote to Karl Gerhardt in 1883, "upon his head is the guilt of only
about one tenth of it, and upon your heads and mine and the rest
of the white race lies fairly and justly the other nine tenths of the
guilt."[90] In a recent book, Terrell Dempsey argues that the writer
often gravitated in memory to comforting lies about the treatment of slaves in his boyhood home. Such was the pressure of
guilt that it enforced flight to the happy fictions of *Tom Sawyer*
and "Old Times on the Mississippi." But "Hannibal was never the

sleepy white town of Clemens's childhood idyl," Dempsey argues, "but instead a place of turmoil, which increased as the nation slid into civil war." Young Sam Clemens was never far from the eye of the storm. He came from a slave-holding family; his father was a leading actor in the local struggle against abolitionists; and the newspaper to which he was apprenticed in 1848 was vigorously partisan. Little wonder that guilt fell so heavily upon him when he was finally at liberty to see clearly what he had formerly strained to ignore and deny: little wonder that he held himself responsible for white crimes against black slaves. "For a man with as big a conscience as Sam Clemens's," Dempsey concludes, "it must have been a terrible burden."[91]

Mark Twain made public business of his guilt about slavery— and about many other things—but he kept his views on sex almost entirely to himself. Guy Cardwell is insightful about what he describes as "the neurotically puritanical side of Clemens's ambivalence toward sexuality"[92] In the same vein, Justin Kaplan observes that for Twain "the loss of sexual innocence . . . was the equivalent of a total collapse of morality. . . . He was notoriously reticent about depicting mature sexual and emotional relationships."[93] Such fastidiousness is undoubtedly geared to the interplay of Twain's stern Presbyterian religious training with the relatively freewheeling mores of young male experience on the western frontier, whether in the Missouri of his youth or the California and Nevada of his early manhood. But just as Freud's central preoccupation with sex is obliquely inflected with repressed personal guilt, Twain's central preoccupation with guilt, and most especially with guilt about race-slavery, is obliquely inflected with repressed memories of formative sexual experience. The evidence for this claim is his extraordinary 1897 notebook account of a dream involving a "negro wench."

> She was very vivid to me—round black face, shiny black eyes, thick lips, very white regular teeth showing through her smile. She was about 22, and plump—not fleshy, not fat, merely rounded and plump; and good-natured and not at all bad-looking. She had but one garment on—a coarse tow-linen shirt that reached

from her neck to her ankles without break. She sold me a pie; a mushy apple pie—hot. She was eating one herself with a tin teaspoon. She made a disgusting proposition to me—for I was young (I was never old in a dream yet) and it seemed quite natural that it should come from her. It was disgusting, but I did not say so; I merely made a chafing remark, brushing aside the matter—a little jeeringly—and this embarrassed her and she made an awkward pretence that I had misunderstood her. I made a sarcastic remark about this pretence, and asked for a spoon to eat my pie with. She had but the one, and she took it out of her mouth, in a quite matter-of-course way, and offered it to me. My stomach rose—there everything vanished. (*MTN* 351 52)

There is no suggestion here of the kind of self-consciousness that we glimpsed in Freud's charged narrative about Irma. Twain's forbidden erotic fantasy so successfully eludes the censors as to leave no trace of the guilt that enforces its repression. Had the writer seen what his notebook entry so clearly reveals, he would not have committed it to paper in the first place. The contrast between the sexually saturated description of the "negro wench" and "My Platonic Sweetheart," Twain's 1898 account of his perfectly chaste dream encounters with a virginal white girl—"I have never known her to shame herself with an impropriety of conduct or utter a speech which I should not be willing that all the world might hear," he declares[94]—is profoundly telling. The "negro wench" is at once irresistible and dangerous for the dreamer because she embodies the unspeakable sexual allure of black women for white men in American slave culture. As scholars have been quick to observe, the novelist grew up in a society that looked the other way when it came to the sexual exploitation of slave girls by young white men.[95] For Twain, the adult sequel to a southern upbringing was sexual prudishness driven in some significant degree by reflex recoil from guilty memories and persistent upwellings of repressed interracial desire. As I have observed, Twain gives no signs of a conscious awareness of this fissure in his psyche. Yet it is surely evidence of an unconscious prompting toward such a reckoning that his account of the "negro wench" dream is immediately preceded in the same notebook entry by his discussion of split consciousness—and conscience—in Stevenson's *Dr. Jekyll and Mr. Hyde.* The very blandness of his rendering of the dream testifies to the depths to which its guilty significance has been banished.

While repressed links between guilt and sex are thus discernible in the work of both writers, the first category is nonetheless broader and more central for Twain, just as the second is broader and more central for Freud. This is not to suggest, of course, that Freud in any way minimized the authority of guilt. October 15, 1897, marks the day on which he announced in a letter his "discovery" of the Oedipus complex. In the same letter, to his most intimate intellectual confidant, Wilhelm Fleiss, he speculates that Hamlet's enigmatic reluctance to take revenge arises from an inward remorse for having once desired the death of his father. In Freud's succinct formulation: "His conscience is his unconscious sense of guilt."[96] Years later, his conception of the superego took its rise from the same potently formative intersection of sex and aggression. When children renounce their universal erotic and aggressive designs on their parents, Freud argues, they internalize and direct toward themselves the prohibitions to which they have surrendered. "The more powerful the Oedipus complex," he goes on, "and the more rapidly it succumbed to repression (under the influence of authority, religious teaching, schooling and reading), the stricter will be the domination of the super-ego over the ego later on—in the form of conscience or perhaps of an unconscious sense of guilt."[97] Supercharged by the energy of the id, and making no distinction between wrongs merely imagined and wrongs in deed, the superego emerges as the leading agent of irrational human suffering.

Mark Twain, quite obviously, endured a similar, though even more intense, vulnerability to guilt. Leading elements in his childhood experience—his resentment of his father, his love of his mother, and his exposure to a severe Presbyterian moral regime during an impressionable period—form the background to the humorist's adult subjection to a truly predatory superego. As we have seen, his conscience appeared to him as an entirely independent, fiercely punitive psychic entity, bent on the infliction of maximum suffering quite without regard to actual misdeeds. It is compelling testimony to the strength of his superego that Twain's conception of it so closely anticipates Freud's, and yet that he surrendered again and again to its domination. He knew exactly what he was up against, yet that knowledge was of scant practical use.

Little wonder that when his brother Henry died in 1858, Twain turned on himself all the repressed aggression that he felt toward the younger sibling who was beloved by everyone, most of all by his mother. His was a textbook case of neurotic mourning, or melancholia, which arises, Freud argues, when the superego becomes "a kind of gathering-place for the death instincts." From the point of view "of instinctual control, of morality," he goes on to explain, "it may be said of the id that it is totally non-moral, of the ego that it strives to be moral, and of the super-ego that it can be super-moral and then become as cruel as only the id can be. It is remarkable that the more a man checks his aggressiveness toward the exterior the more severe—that is aggressive—he becomes in his ego ideal."[98] Aggressive indeed! "O, God! this is hard to bear," wrote the afflicted Twain to his sister-in-law. "Hardened, hopeless—aye, lost—lost—lost and ruined sinner as I am—I, even *I*, have humbled my self to the ground and prayed as never man prayed before, that the great God might let this cup pass from me—that he would strike me to the earth, but spare my brother—that he would pour out the fulness of his just wrath upon my wicked head, but have mercy, mercy, mercy upon that unoffending boy."[99]

According to Freud, we are born guilty. Because the universal Oedipal conflict recapitulates the murder by his sons of the primal father—the event "with which civilization began and which, since it occurred, has not allowed mankind a moment's rest"[100]—we are always already burdened with an unconscious endowment of ancient guilt. Our load is increased during the course of life as repressed aggressive instincts are internalized, appropriated by the superego, and then directed back, all their harshness intact, upon the ego. "The tension between the harsh super-ego and the ego that is subjected to it," Freud explains, "is called the sense of guilt; it expresses itself as a need for punishment."[101] This is of course the conscience as Twain experienced and understood it: powerful, autonomous, relentless, launching guerrilla attacks against the ego from the secret depths of the unconscious, with the aim of punishing not only what we do, but what we think we might like to do.

But the similarity between the two men on this pivotal issue goes deeper still. For both bore witness to the fact that human beings experience guilt not only as the result of their misdeeds, but also in advance of them. In "Criminals from a Sense of Guilt," Freud concludes from analytical observation that an oppressive sense of guilt is often the cause, and not the consequence, of human wrongdoing. "Paradoxical as it may sound," he notes, "I must maintain that the sense of guilt was present before the misdeed, that it did not arise from it, but conversely—the misdeed arose from the sense of guilt."[102] Guilt runs before deeds, Freud contends, because "it is an expression of the conflict due to ambivalence, of the eternal struggle between Eros and the instinct of destruction or death"—a struggle manifest in the primal act of patricide, and in human subjection ever since to the gathering authority of the superego. Anticipatory mental stress is also a feature of Freud's developed understanding of anxiety, which is triggered by a variety of instinctive and repressed impulses that give rise in consciousness to a feeling of helpless vulnerability to real or imagined, known or unknown perils. As succinctly summarized by Peter Gay, "Anxiety is a monitory report that there is danger ahead."[103]

Freud turns to Ibsen's *Rosmersholm* for a dramatic illustration of anticipatory guilt. Driven by a passion for her employer, Johannes Rosmer, Rebecca Gamvik successfully schemes to remove his wife from the scene, but then surrenders to an inner voice of conscience that forbids the completion of her conquest. Rebecca's guilt arises when she learns that she is actually the daughter of her former employer, Dr. West, who adopted her after her mother's death. This is especially crippling information because she had an affair with Dr. West before she knew that she was his illegitimate child. However, it is vitally important that Rebecca declines to marry Rosmer *before* she has knowledge of her incestuous relationship with her father. For as Freud observes, "the sense of guilt which bids her renounce the fruit of her actions is thus effective before she knows anything of her cardinal crime." The enigmatic influence of Rebecca's conscience is clear evidence, Freud goes on to argue, of "the domination of the Oedipus complex, even though she did not know that this universal phantasy had in her case become a reality."[104]

It comes as no surprise that Freud traces Rebecca's "obscure sense of guilt before the deed"[105] to an unconscious sexual origin. Quite as predictably, the dozens of instances of what I have described elsewhere as "proleptic guilt" in Twain's work are premonitions—amply freighted with ambivalence and anxiety—of future misdeeds anticipated in earlier moral lapses of thought or action, rarely if ever sexual in nature.[106] The *locus classicus* of such baffling attacks of conscience appears in the first chapter of *Huckleberry Finn*, when the young narrator, weary with the rigors of civilized life at the home of the Widow Douglas, withdraws to his room.

> Then I set down in a chair by the window and tried to think of something cheerful, but it warn't no use. I felt so lonesome I most wished I was dead. The stars was shining, and the leaves rustled in the woods ever so mournful; and I heard an owl, away off, who-whooing about somebody that was dead, and a whippowill and a dog crying about somebody that was going to die; and the wind was trying to whisper something to me and I couldn't make out what it was, and so it made the cold shivers run over me. Then away out in the woods I heard that kind of a sound that a ghost makes when it wants to tell about something that's on its mind and can't make itself understood, and so can't rest easy in its grave and has to go about that way every night, grieving. I got so downhearted and scared, I did wish I had some company. (*HF* 4)

The key elements common to this passage, and to many others like it in Twain's writing, are feelings of loneliness, life-weariness, and the wish to die, accompanied by soft, haunting sounds, which seem to be the voices of ghosts seeking compassion and murmuring about death. These recurrent forebodings are almost invariably geared to the workings of conscience, and more particularly to the stirrings of guilt emerging in advance of the events which will properly give them rise. In Huck's case, those events are the many occasions in the subsequent narrative when his profound ambivalence about his black companion, Jim, triggers acts of betrayal, large and small. His painful anxiety, as he sits haunted and alone in his room, thus anticipates the guilt he will experience again and again in the course of their journey together.

Huck's guilt has its foundation in an ambivalence about race that reflects the culture of his community, and that he shares with his maker. But though morally fraught memories of slavery were perhaps preeminent among the spurs to Twain's conscience, there were many items on what he described to Howells as "my list of permanencies—a list of humiliations that extends back to when I was seven years old, & which keep on persecuting me regardless of my repentancies" (*MTHL* 1:212). His guilty premonitions of his brother Henry's death—which expressed an ambivalence with an unconscious fratricidal wish as one of its poles—is fictionally reprised in the proleptic guilt experienced by Theodor Fischer in *The Mysterious Stranger*. When he learns from Young Satan that his friend Nikolaus is fated to die in twelve days, Theodor's consciousness is flooded with memories of his former mistreatment of his doomed companion. "No, I could not sleep," he complains. "These little shabby wrongs upbraided me and tortured me; and with a pain much sharper than one feels when the wrongs have been done to the living. Nikolaus *was* living, but no matter: he was to me as one already dead. The wind was still moaning about the eaves, the rain still pattering up on the panes" (*MS* 122).

Fretful anxiety, marked ambivalence, solitude, a preoccupation with death, and the drone of mournful, ghostly sounds—the setting and state of mind are the recurrent elements of the proleptic guilt that in Twain's life and work anticipates Freud's later theorizing about "the obscure sense of guilt before the deed." Some of the same elements turn up in "My First Lie and How I Got Out of It," where Twain declares that deceitfulness is by an "eternal law" the very essence of human nature. Since man "didn't invent the law," he is not responsible for its effect; "it is merely his business to obey it and keep still" (*CTSSE* 2:440). Twain defines this act of concealment as "the lie of silent assertion," the mute denial that humans are universally dishonest. Most people come to believe this lie of lies, and actually imagine themselves honest. But Twain includes himself in an enlightened minority of perspicacious witnesses to "the lie of silent assertion." A member of this group—designated "we that know"—stands apart not only in recognizing the operation of "the eternal law" in his nature, but also in bending to that law by deceiving "his fellow-conspirators into imagining that he doesn't know that the law exists. It is what we all do," Twain observes with weary resignation, "we that know" (*CTSSE* 2:440).

Members of this elite understand the dynamics and awesome dominion of unacknowledged (and for most people, unrecognized) deception in human experience. This is knowledge of solemn gravity, for it focuses not on trivial, quotidian deceits, but rather on the ways in which "the lie of silent assertion" has "for ages and ages . . . mutely labored in the interest of despotisms and aristocracies and chattel slaveries, and military slaveries, and religious slaveries, and has kept them alive; keeps them alive yet, here and there and yonder, all about the globe; and will go on keeping them alive until the silent-assertion lie retires from business." Among his examples of modern crimes against humanity, Twain gives first place to American slavery, an institution that fed deeply on lies. "It would not be possible," he insists,

> for a humane and intelligent person to invent a rational excuse for slavery; yet you will remember that in the early days of the emancipation agitation in the North the agitators got but small help or countenance from any one. Argue and plead and pray as they might, they could not break the universal stillness that reigned, from pulpit and press all the way down to the bottom of society—the clammy stillness created and maintained by the lie of silent

assertion—the silent assertion that there wasn't anything going on in which humane and intelligent people were interested.[107]

Proleptic guilt is momentarily perceptible in "the clammy stillness" that accompanies the commission of "the lie of silent assertion" as it bears on American slavery. Twain's childhood immersion in a culture that turned a blind eye to the cruelty and inhumanity of the peculiar institution was the seed from which he reaped great remorse in his adult years. I have elsewhere characterized "the lie of silent assertion" as a species of "bad faith," the deception of self and other in the denial of violations of public ideals of truth and justice. Such departures, as they appear in Twain's work, are most frequently group phenomena, collaborative denials, and they bear with them the clear implication that people will sometimes permit or acquiesce in what they cannot approve, so long as their complicity is submerged in a larger, tacit consensus. Bad faith is not always bad, as it may enable a society to transcend the strict letter of its codes and the unanticipated exigencies of circumstance. But it may also work to conceal problems of grave consequence. Twain was sharply aware of the social unity and fellow feeling to be derived from evasions of the truth, but he was equally attentive to the pathologies they foster and sustain. In either form, however, it is a telling feature of acts of bad faith that they incorporate silent prohibitions against the acknowledgment that they have occurred. Denial is itself denied.

As "My First Lie" clearly demonstrates, Twain was a penetrating analyst of bad faith, most especially as it spread through the culture of American race-slavery. But membership in the elite "we that know" hardly exempted him from the seductions of moral evasion. He was a man devoted to the pleasure principle, after all, and most fervently so when it came to reducing the intolerable stress of conscience. Twain's negotiations in bad faith are everywhere the business of his art. Sometimes, as in "My First Lie," he is the conscious master of his subject. More often, however, his writing dramatizes the struggles of a highly sensitive moral nature in thrall to the tyranny of unconscious guilt. Such half-blind grappling is nowhere better illustrated than in the Bombay section of *Following the Equator*, when a German tourist's callous mistreatment of an Indian servant brings Twain to a startling recognition. "I had not seen the like of this for fifty years. It carried me back to my boyhood, and flashed upon me the forgotten fact that this was the *usual* way of explaining one's desire to a slave." Running darkly through the memories is a burden of guilt that he strains to dispel. He insists that striking slaves "seemed right and natural" when he was a boy, but he cannot deny that he felt "sorry for the victim and ashamed for the punisher."

This furtive, morally troubled train of thought comes partially to rest in a reflexive turn inward on itself, as Twain dilates on the mystery of his own mental processes. "It is curious," he observes, "the space-annihilating power of thought. For just one second, all that goes to make the *me* in me was in a Missourian village, on the other side of the globe, vividly seeing again those forgotten pictures of fifty years ago . . . and in the next second I was back in Bombay, and that kneeling native's smitten cheek was not done tingling yet." There is of course an unacknowledged moral reprieve in the suggestion that consciousness is so rapid and far flung in its movements as to have no fixed place or center. In such a construction of subjectivity, there is no real "*me* in me," and thus no place for guilt to take hold and fester. Thanks to such timely philosophical interventions, an awakened sense of moral anguish is laid at least temporarily to rest. "Then," Twain sighs, "came peace—stillness deep and solemn—and lasted till five."

But of course the self does have a center of sorts, to be found in Twain's case along lines of association linking Bombay to Hannibal, the British Empire to the antebellum American South, and the abused Indian servant to the suffering slave. In both settings, separated by half a world, half a century, and only "two seconds by the clock," Twain is witness to an uncanny repetition of events from which he draws back in horror. Stung by painful intimations of his own complicity, he retreats to the imagined moral shelter of youth, ignorance, and solipsism, only to find that in none of these is he safe from blame. And so the backpedaling into denial continues with the portrait of the Indian crow whose raucous screeching brings an end to sleep and a return to the stress of consciousness. The bird is a protean rascal who in the course of numberless reincarnations has been guilty of all possible sins. Thanks to this "sublime march toward ultimate perfection," he is "the hardest lot that wears feathers. Yes, and the cheerfulest, and the best satisfied with himself." Little wonder that the conscience-stricken traveler is drawn to the crow, who has trumped guilt with indifference. "He does not know what care is," observes an admiring Twain; "he does not know what sorrow is, he does not know what remorse is, his life is one long thundering ecstasy of happiness, and he will go to his death untroubled, knowing that he will soon turn up again as an author or something, and be even more intolerably capable and comfortable than ever he was before" (FE 351–56).[108]

Mark Twain's writing reflects in manifold direct and indirect ways his lifelong subjection to relentless, punishing guilt. The problem was intensely personal with him; it bled into his work. There is no answering idiosyncrasy in Freud's writing. He was preoccupied with human sexuality, to be sure, but his emphasis was largely clinical and theoretical. Freud was of course closely attentive to guilt, especially in his second theory of the psyche, in which the superego emerges in the role of judge or censor to the ego. But while conscience in this guise is fiercely punitive, the context of its operation is remote from the Christian battle-ground of good and evil in which Twain made his way. Freud-ian guilt, observes Phillip Rieff, is "a psychological not a moral fact."[109] We experience guilt because we repress instinctual de-sires; the solution, Freud insists, is a reduction in our unrealistic moral aspirations. While they were at one in tracing the tyranny of conscience to the exigencies of modern civilization, Twain in-habited a world of moral cripples, Freud of neurotics.

This is not to deny that Freud's construction of psychological reality is compatible with the operations of bad faith as Twain understood and embodied them. As Jonathan Lear points out, Freud makes ample provision for the kind of motivated irratio-nality everywhere on display in bad faith.[110] We choose to deny what we know, and to banish it from consciousness, because we find it disagreeable. Thus Huck tries to forget what he knows about the snake skins. Freud also agreed with Twain that such denial is often incomplete, and that it is entirely possible for people to know and to unknow the same thing. A repressed idea or image can enter consciousness on condition that it is modified to elude censorship; just so, Huck is vexed by constant, unsummoned reminders of the snake skins. Both writers recognized from personal experience that impulses to deny and conceal often operate in tension with countering impulses to confess and reveal. Twain the author-cat knew that he could not keep his own secrets, while Freud in *The Interpretation of Dreams* is evidently torn between conflicting inclinations, "largely underground," in the view of Peter Gay, toward "self revelation and self-protection."[111] Both knew as well, of course, that the unconscious figures prominently in all such complex psychological processes.

But because Freud gave conventional morality much less credence than Twain, he gave much less specific attention to what I have called bad faith, the impulse and the mechanisms involved in the denial of personal lapses from virtue. Freud emphasizes that the instinctual renunciation demanded in civilized society makes a "hypocrite" of the individual, "whether he is clearly aware of the incongruity or not."[112] But he presses the case largely in terms of the unnatural conditions giving rise to the problem, and not to the specifics of its expression. Nor is there anything narrowly moral in Freud's broad definition of repression—a mental operation whose "motive and purpose [is] nothing else than the avoidance of unpleasure"[113]—or in his understanding of disavowal and resistance. True, the psychic fissure first fully elaborated in *The Ego and the Id*—"an unconscious sense of guilt," split off from and yet governed by the ego[114]—is compatible in theory with the operations of bad-faith denial as Twain represents and embodies them. But Freud is interested in the ego's unconscious suppression of guilt as an obstacle to recovery, not as a mechanism of moral evasion.

Their differences in emphasis notwithstanding, Freud and Twain were in complete agreement that the hypertrophy of guilt in modern life had reached dangerous levels. Reflecting on the unhappiness wrought by the dominance of the superego, Freud

speculates ruefully that "the whole of mankind [may] have become neurotic."[115] Between bouts of surrender to irrational guilt,
Twain was tireless in reminding readers (and himself) that their
bondage to necessity frees human beings from moral responsibility for their sins. "God," he insisted time and again, "is unquestionably responsible for every foreknown or unforeknown crime
committed by man, his creature."[116] Twain's resort to determinism was extreme, but so was its corollary, a bottomless disenchantment with "the blacknesses and rottennesses" of human
nature, his own included.[117] Freud's assessment was only slightly
less bleak. As he surveyed "the vast amount of brutality, cruelty
and lies" unleashed by the Great War, he concluded that human
aggression "is an original, self-subsisting instinctual disposition
in man," and it "constitutes the greatest impediment to civilization."[118]

In a world naturally inclined to its own destruction, the restraints of civilization are imperative. Neither Freud nor Twain
warmed to the idea of political revolution; both bent to the
need for strong authority. Yet for both, civilization was a necessary evil whose excesses threatened consequences no less dire
and ignominious than those attendant on unrestrained barbarism. Both, that is, bore witness to a world caught in a possibly
fatal dilemma. Such is the argument of Freud's *Civilization and
Its Discontents*. Escape from a Hobbesian state of nature entails
renunciation of unrestrained instinctual pleasures. As the result,
"the sexual life of civilized man is . . . severely impaired" to the
point that its yield of happiness "has sensibly diminished." Civilizing Eros is also obstructed in its unifying mission by aggressive
instincts that pit each against all. But harnessing aggression has
its own grave peril, for it results in the formation of the superego, which directs inward against the self all the harsh aggressiveness formerly channeled outward against others. As Freud puts
it, "Civilization . . . obtains mastery over the individual's dangerous desire for aggression by weakening and disarming it and by
setting up an agency within him to watch over it, like a garrison
in a conquered city." Once inside the gates, the superego, drawing
on the legacy of primordial Oedipal guilt and on the momentum

of its own success, achieves such complete domination that it in turn becomes the chief threat to the fruition of human wishes. "What a potent obstacle to civilization aggressiveness must be," Freud observes with dismay, "if the defence against it can cause as much unhappiness as aggressiveness itself!"[119] And so he leaves us, spectators to the unresolved struggle of love and hate in a civilization menaced by the specter of Adolf Hitler.

Writing more than a generation earlier, Mark Twain looked on with increasing disgust at the colonial predations of the world's leading industrial powers. He sailed around the world in 1896, taking a course though all of the major outposts of the vast British Empire. It was a sobering look at brutal domination driven by the arrogant assumption that "the world was made for man— the white man" (FE 185). Next it was American misadventures in Cuba and the Philippines, which shattered all his illusions about his nation's honorable immunity to the shameful race for colonial possessions. Twain took arms against the outrage in essays such as "To the Person Sitting in Darkness" and "A Defense of General Funston," and in "The Secret History of Eddypus," a nightmare vision of the American empire of the future in which he allows that

> civilization is an elusive and baffling term. . . . In America and Europe it seems to have meant benevolence, gentleness, godliness, justice, magnanimity, purity, love, and we gather that men considered it a duty to confer it as a blessing upon all lowly and harmless peoples of remote regions; but as soon as it was transplanted it became a blight, a pestilence, an awful terror, and they whom it was sent to benefit fled from its presence imploring their pagan gods with tears and lamentations to save them from it. The strength of such evidence as has come down to us seems to indicate that it was a sham at home and only laid off its disguise when abroad.[120]

Twain's world, like Freud's, was threatened by rising tides of aggression; but it was threatened as well by the restraints deemed necessary to their control. Twain would have agreed completely with Freud's conclusion that "the price we pay for our advance in civilization is a loss of happiness through the heightening of the sense of guilt."[121] "Civilization *is* Repression," he instructed his secretary, Isabel Lyon, in 1905. She concurred emphatically: "You have to jam down out of sight the action of the strongest laws of your being and the great cry of truth."[122] Aggression was part of the equation, as we have seen, deplorable of course, but natural, and irresistibly the source of pleasure. "The joy of killing! the joy of seeing killing done," Twain acknowledged, "these are the traits of the human race at large. We white people are merely modified Thugs; Thugs fretting under the restraints of a not very thick skin of civilization" (*FE* 437).

Eros also figured prominently in Twain's moral calculus, though he wrote little about it until late in his life. His own hesitation was of course part and parcel of the unnatural restrictions on sexual expression that he ridiculed in civilized behavior. In "Eve's Diary," the mother of mankind admits that she loves Adam not for his estimable moral qualities, but "because he is *mine*, and is *masculine*." "It is a matter of sex," she concludes.[123] But Eve's natural pleasure in sex gives way in civilization to a severely straitened moral regime in which the body is viewed as a vessel of depravity. In "Letters from the Earth," when Satan reports on what he sees as man's generalized derangement, he notes that it expresses itself most clearly in a "grotesque" conception of heaven that includes—"I give you my word," Satan swears—"not a single feature . . . that he *actually values*." The chief casualty in this sweeping renunciation of pleasure is, of course, sex. Man "has imagined a heaven," Satan reports, "and has left entirely out of it the supremest of all his delights, the one ecstasy that stands first and foremost in the heart of every individual of his race—and ours—sexual intercourse."[124]

Driven by instincts that they can neither completely resist nor approve, civilized human beings are, in Twain's view, as in Freud's, caught in a bind that makes them easy prey to the tyranny of conscience. For the Viennese doctor, the superego was an obstacle to human happiness so obdurate as to threaten the survival of the species. For the aging American humorist, the coupling in their nature of a rigid demand for self-approval with constitutional, even predetermined, defects of moral character compels civilized human beings to seek relief from crippling self-accusation in bad-faith denial. Moral evasion—"the lie of silent assertion" —in turn diverts attention away from, and thereby sustains and abets, the very social pathologies, such as race-slavery, that trigger the initiating spasm of conscience. For both, then, civilized renunciation of instinctual pleasures is accompanied by the rise of a moral regime so punishing as to threaten the health and, indeed, the future of society. The problem: guilt; the solution: less of it. This is Huck's view, of course; it is shared by Hank Morgan, the hero of *A Connecticut Yankee in King Arthur's Court*. "If I had the remaking of man," Hank reflects, "he wouldn't have any conscience. It is one of the most disagreeable things connected with a person; and although it certainly does a great deal of good, it cannot be said to pay, in the long run; it would be much better to have less good and more comfort" (*CY* 219). Where Nietzsche would have had less good and more uninhibited power of self-creation, Freud agreed, less heroically and more prosaically, with Twain— insisting that most people "would have been more healthy if it could have been possible for them to be less good."[125]

The striking affinity between our writers expresses itself at a more abstract level in what I will refer to as their presiding myths, the grand narratives that serve as compressed, informing points of origin for their more diffuse and detailed representations of human experience. These are the big stories from which the little ones take their rise and shape. Freud's myth is the better known. It is of course the tragic story of Oedipus, the young man whose cruel fate it is to murder his father and sleep with his mother. In *Totem and Taboo*, Freud expands this ancient narrative into a founding myth in which a band of brothers murder and cannibalize their tyrannical father, who has forbidden them access to all sexual privileges. Because their hatred of their father is mingled with love, the sons are overtaken by remorse and the superego is born, and along with it a civilization burdened with a legacy of ambivalence and unconscious guilt. It matters not at all that most modern men refrain from patricide, Freud argues. "One is bound to feel guilty in either case, for the sense of guilt is an expression of the conflict due to ambivalence, of the eternal struggle between Eros and the instinct of destruction or death."[126]

The same elements figure centrally in the much less familiar myth that presides in Twain's writing. It is also a story of family conflict, not between sons and their father, but between brothers. Fierce love and hate drive the action toward a tragic denouement that leaves unbearable guilt—at first conscious, but subsequently unconscious—in its wake. It is a myth, like Freud's, woven into the fabric of an entire culture. The Oedipal narrative is principally concerned with resistance to authority. It is a story appropriate to a late nineteenth-century Austrian, and indeed European, civilization in the throes of conflict between old despotism and a new, liberal vision of freedom and dignity for all. By contrast, Twain's myth focuses on conflict between brothers leading toward betrayal and catastrophe. It is redolent not of classical myth, but of the biblical story of Cain and Abel, which, Satan observes in *The Mysterious Stranger,* marks the point of origin for civilization (*MS* 134).[127] It is a narrative entirely apposite to a nation that pitted brother against brother in a bloody civil war, and that continued, in the aftermath of that conflict, to struggle with the guilty legacy of its historical entanglement in race-slavery.

This American story is unfamiliar because it resurfaces in our midst against considerable resistance. It is a story not so much told as endured in brief snatches and fragments that are no sooner glimpsed than expelled from sight and mind. Twain told the story over and over again without quite knowing what he had done, which is why he was compelled to repeat it. Recall the warning—deeply in earnest, for all of its jocular tone—at the beginning of *Huckleberry Finn:* "Persons attempting to find a motive in this narrative will be prosecuted; persons attempting to find a moral in it will be banished; persons attempting to find a plot in it will be shot" (xxv). Twain had written powerfully in his book about the failure of a noble attempt by a black man and a white boy to escape from the curse of slavery. They are brothers on a raft, and

they fail because their love for each other is interfused with suspicion and animus. They are the sons of Adam and Eve, haunted
and harried by buried memories of snakes.

Mark Twain denied in bad faith the somber thrust of his narrative; he liked to think that he had written about the triumph of
a "sound heart" over a "deformed conscience," and most of his
readers have liked to think the same thing.[128] But bad-faith denial has a reflex impulse to disclosure as its opposite pole. That
is why the hard truth of the novel is discernible, albeit somewhat
darkly, to readers chastened by the American experience in the
late twentieth century; and it is why Twain had to tell the story all over again, denying its grave implications as he did so, in
"unreadable" narratives such as *Pudd'nhead Wilson*, and in now-
forgotten fragments like "Tom Sawyer's Conspiracy" and "Which
Was It?" both of which were terminated in bad-faith resistance to
their drift toward the guilty truth.[129]

The American myth according to Mark Twain, unlike the Freudian version of the Oedipal story, was intensely personal to its teller.
It surfaces first in his account of the death of his brother, Henry,
in 1858, which precipitated an assault of guilt-laden pathological
mourning—the yield on an ambivalence with a dark, fratricidal
pole—from which the survivor never recovered. But the theme
of fraternal betrayal had roots quite as deep in Twain's childhood
experience with slaves, in which affection and respect mingled
uneasily with racial condescension and the anguished murmur-
ings of conscience—of proleptic guilt—in the face of undeniable
iniquity. Hence the deep division in his psyche between impulses
to deny and to reveal the unbearable truth about himself and his
world, a division with its creative correlative in a compulsive preoccupation with fraternal pairs—pairs including Tom and Sid,
Tom and Injun Joe, Huck and Tom, Huck and Jim, Chang and
Eng, Tom Canty and Edward Tudor, Luigi and Angelo Capello,
Tom Driscoll and Valet de Chambre, Theodor Fischer and Nikolaus Baumann, August Feldner and No. 44, and many others—
who are impelled by conflicted feelings of love and hate toward
betrayal, catastrophe, guilt, and denial. Hence as well Twain's
gravitation to the uncanny, which we have already observed in

Pudd'nhead Wilson, but which is widely manifest in his writing. Freud's account of the frightening phenomenon aligns closely in numerous and striking ways with the dynamics of the bad faith everywhere at large in Twain's work. The uncanny, Freud writes, is to be found in association with "a doubling, dividing and interchanging of the self"; with the superego, itself divided from the ego and charged with "observing and criticizing the self"; and with the compulsion to return in consciousness to "something which is familiar and well-established in the mind and which has become alienated from it only through the process of repression." Some of these elements, Freud is pleased to observe, coalesce in an "irresistibly comic" episode in *A Tramp Abroad*.[130] But they are more frequently found in situations where fraternal betrayal and repressed guilt, the staples of Twain's emergent American myth, powerfully intersect.

This occurs most memorably, perhaps, in "Which Was It?" a painfully autobiographical dream narrative in which George Harrison, a man blessed by fortune with wealth, reputation, and a happy home, loses it all when he falls into a guilt-ridden nightmare of debt and family disgrace. This was Twain's disastrous 1894 bankruptcy as it appeared to him toward the end of his life. But there is yet more to be told in a narrative so impossibly convoluted as to suggest that it was written under moral duress, but with an answering and unconscious desire that it *not* be read, let alone understood. Entangled in a web of murder and deception, Harrison takes refuge in moral evasions, but is prey nonetheless to near-suicidal remorse. Accusing memories "flocked to the front as fast as they were banished, and with every return they seemed to come refreshed and reinforced for their bitter work upon his conscience." He commences his final descent into complete self-loathing when Jasper, a twice-enslaved, twice-self-liberated free black man surfaces abruptly, as if from nowhere, into the story. Jasper's advent is sudden and shocking because he is the possessor of carefully guarded evidence that Harrison is guilty of murder. This is his leverage on his white master. Even more significantly, Jasper is a stubborn reminder of the guilt for the crime of slavery deeply repressed in the white psyche. His principal motive is to seek a just reprisal for the generations of brutal mistreatment and injustice endured by his people. "Dey's a long bill agin de lowdown ornery white race," he lectures Harrison, "en you's a-gwyneter to *settle* it."[131] Harrison's penalty is to changes places with a lowly slave and thus to experience firsthand the pain and humiliation that he once imposed, with unruffled moral complacency, on other human beings. When Jasper forces his white hostage to change places, he gives outward expression to yet another subversive secret, the much deeper interchangeability of their identities. As the son of a slave woman and her master, Harrison's uncle, Jasper is blood kin; and as a party to Harrison's most guardedly guilty secrets, he is the white man's psychological double, his avenging conscience, that "something," in Freud's understanding of the uncanny, "which ought to have remained hidden but has come to light."[132]

Jasper is the black brother betrayed, returning in a nightmare from which his white brother cannot awaken, to deliver the guilty truth at the heart of Mark Twain's myth of America. Harrison can no more reawaken to easeful domestic prosperity than he can endure the nightmare of guilt and retribution into which he has fallen. No sooner has he persuaded himself, in textbook bad faith, that his "troubles" are all in his head, that "it is the mind that manufactures them, and the mind can forget them, banish them, abolish them,"[133] than Jasper arrives to confront him with the very reality he has been straining blindly to expel from consciousness. They are brothers under the skin, alienated by generations of cruelty, suffering, and denial, and now pitted against one another, retributive rage on one side, desperate bad-faith denial on the other. It is of course integral to the meaning of the story that the author is no more successful than his protagonist in escaping from the narrative's plunge into darkness. Thus even as it dramatizes the hopeless bad faith of its leading characters, "Which Was It?" betrays symptomatic resistance to its own powerful critique of American slave culture. Harrison's uncanny encounter with his dark double is recapitulated in Twain's baffled compulsion to commence yet again, and yet again to deny, the tragic narrative of fraternal love and hate that rose, as if by a mind of its own, from the guilty core of his creativity. He was as powerless to proscribe his generative myth from consciousness as he was to resolve it when it flowed, yet once more unsummoned, from his pen. This would be Faulkner's challenge, and America's.

NOTES

1. Mark Twain, autobiographical dictation, September 4, 1907, MTP.

2. Sigmund Freud to Lothar Bickel, June 28, 1931, as quoted in Peter Gay, *Freud: A Life for Our Time* (New York: Norton, 1988), 46.

3. Carl Dolmetsch, *"Our Famous Guest": Mark Twain in Vienna* (Athens: University of Georgia Press, 1992), 265. Dolmetsch goes on to add that the two "were indisputably in each other's presence—that is in the same room together—on at least two occasions."

4. See, for example, the approving references in "On the History of the Psycho-Analytic Movement," in *SE,* 14:35; "The Uncanny," in *SE,* 17:237; and *Civilization and Its Discontents,* in *SE,* 21:126n2. Freud wrote to Wilhelm Fleiss on February 9, 1898, of having attended a public reading by Mark Twain (*The Complete Letters of Sigmund Freud to Wilhelm Fleiss 1887–1904,* trans. and ed. Jeffrey Moussaleff Masson [Cambridge: Harvard University Press, 1985], 299).

5. Ralph Waldo Emerson, "Life and Letters in New England," in *The American Transcendentalists. Their Prose and Poetry,* ed. Perry Miller (Garden City, NY: Doubleday, 1957), 5–7.

6. Gay, *Freud,* 129.

7. *Mark Twain in Eruption,* ed. Bernard DeVoto (New York: Harper and Brothers, 1940), 119–30. According to Henri F. Ellenberger (*The Discovery of the Unconscious: The History and Evolution of Dynamic Psychiatry* [New York: Basic Books, 1970], 82), Franz Anton Mesmer's influence spread northward from New Orleans in the 1840s. Among its early practitioners was Phineas Parkhurst Quimby, whose patient Mary Baker Eddy was later the object of Twain's critical scrutiny in *Christian Science,* published in 1907.

8. Mark Twain, *Mark Twain's Notebooks and Journals,* vol. 1, *1855–1873,* ed. Frederick Anderson, Michael B. Frank, and Kenneth M. Sanderson (Berkeley: University of California Press, 1975), 21–23. The editors provide a detailed analysis of Twain's treatment of his source, the Reverend George Sumner Weaver's *Lectures on Mental Science according to the Philosophy of Phrenology* (1852).

9. Mark Twain, "My Platonic Sweetheart," 11, unabridged manuscript version, MTP.

10. Mark Twain, "Mental Telegraphy," in *CTSSE*, 1:36. Twain overcame his initial reservations and published the essay in 1891.

11. See "The Spiritual Seance" (1866), in *CTSSE*, 1:199–204. On the Fox sisters and spiritism, see Ellenberger, *Discovery of the Unconscious*, 83–84.

12. Justin Kaplan, *Mr. Clemens and Mark Twain*, 338; Hamlin Hill, *Mark Twain God's Fool*, 33–34.

13. On Myers, see Ellenberger, *Discovery of the Unconscious*, 173–74, 313–14.

14. Samuel L. Clemens to Olivia L. Clemens, January 27–30, 1894, MTP.

15. See Ellenberger, *Discovery of the Unconscious*, 85–90, 145–47, and 311–12.

16. I am gratefully indebted to Susan Gillman for her thorough treatment of Twain's involvement in the revolutionary new psychology of the late nineteenth century. In her *Dark Twins: Imposture and Identity in Mark Twain's America* (Chicago: University of Chicago Press, 1989), Gillman skillfully profiles the intellectual context in which Twain speculated about hypnosis, thought transference, mind cure, and dream analysis. She is aware, as I am, that earlier scholars—notably biographers Justin Kaplan and Hamlin Hill, and pioneering editors John S. Tuckey and William M. Gibson—were academic pioneers in this area of study. More recently, Carl Dolmetsch has richly enhanced our understanding of Twain's immersion in the intellectual and cultural life of fin-de-siècle Vienna.

17. In the shaping of this brief overview, I have drawn most especially on Ellenberger, *Discovery of the Unconscious;* Peter Gay's superb biography, *Freud: A Life for Our Time;* and the indispensable work of J. Laplanche and J.-B. Pontalis, *The Language of Psychoanalysis*, trans. Donald Nicholson-Smith (New York: Norton, 1973).

18. Freud, *Civilization and Its Discontents*, in *SE*, 21:75, 86.

19. Twain, autobiographical dictation, June 19–25, 1906, MTP.

20. For a much fuller development of this vital issue, see my essay "An 'Unconscious and Profitable Cerebration': Mark Twain and Literary Intentionality," *Nineteenth-Century Literature* 50 (1995): 357–80.

21. For more on this topic, see John Forrester, *Truth Games: Lies, Money, and Psychoanalysis* (Cambridge: Harvard University Press, 1997), 69–72.

22. *Complete Letters of Freud to Fleiss*, 272.

23. Sigmund Freud, "Delusions and Dreams in Jensen's *Gradiva*," in *SE*, 9:91–92, 8.

24. Sigmund Freud, *Introductory Lectures on Psychoanalysis*, in *SE*, 16:285.

25. Frank J. Sulloway, *Freud, Biologist of the Mind: Beyond the Psychoanalytic Legend* (Cambridge: Harvard University Press, 1992), 32.

26. Freud, "Negation," in *SE*, 19:239. For more, see Jacques Sédat, *Freud*, trans. Susan Fairfield (New York: Other Press, 2005), 123–24.

27. Sigmund Freud, "The Unconscious," in *SE*, 14:187.

28. Sigmund Freud, "Thoughts for the Times on War and Death," in *SE*, 14:296.

29. Twain, "My Platonic Sweetheart," 11–12, 27–29, 34, MTP.

30. Gillman, *Dark Twins*, 163. No. 44, the eponymous hero of the narrative, belatedly reveals that he is the "creature" of his host August Feldner's dreams and possesses all the qualities Twain associated with the unconscious. "With my race," No. 44 explains, "it is different; we have no limits of any kind, we comprehend all things." By comparison, mortal consciousness is decidedly inferior. "You see, for your race there is such a thing as *time*—you cut it up and measure it. . . . To your race there is also such a thing as *distance*—and, hang it, you measure *that*, too! . . . Can't you extinguish time?" he asks, knowing full well that the answer is no; "*can't* you comprehend eternity?" (*MS* 331–32).

31. For an excellent, critically far-reaching discussion of the issues raised here, see Susan K. Harris, *Mark Twain's Escape from Time* (Columbia: University of Missouri Press, 1982).

32. Sigmund Freud, *The Interpretation of Dreams*, in *SE*, 4:160.

33. Mark Twain, *Which Was the Dream?* ed. John S. Tuckey (Berkeley: University of California Press, 1966), 1–7.

34. Samuel L. Clemens to Joseph H. Twichell, July 28, 1904, MTP.

35. Freud, "Thoughts for the Times on War and Death," in *SE*, 14:297.

36. Gay, *Freud*, 128.

37. Twain, "The Facts Concerning the Recent Carnival of Crime in Connecticut," in *CTSSE*, 1:660.

38. Terrell Dempsey, *Searching for Jim: Slavery in Sam Clemens's World* (Columbia: University of Missouri Press, 2003), 221–24.

39. Sigmund Freud, *Moses and Monotheism*, in *SE*, 23:124–27.

40. Sigmund Freud, "Fragment of an Analysis of a Case of Hysteria," in *SE*, 7:77–78.

41. Samuel L. Clemens to William Dean Howells, March 14, 1904, in *MTHL* 2:782. In a 1904 autobiographical dictation, "A Memory of John Hay," Twain reports that Hay believed that an autobiographer "*will* tell the truth in spite of himself, for his facts and his fictions will work loyally together for the protection of the reader; each fact and each fiction will be a dab of paint, each will fall in its right place, and together they will paint his portrait; not the portrait *he* thinks they are painting, but his real portrait, the inside of him, the soul of him, his character" (MTP).

42. Tom is likewise convinced that Becky Thatcher's "face" will betray her secrets (see *The Adventures of Tom Sawyer*, ed. John C. Gerber, Paul Baender, and Terry Firkins [Berkeley: University of California Press, 1980], 156).

43. Freud, "The Uncanny," in *SE*, 17:247.

44. For a much fuller exploration of this topic, see Gillman, *Dark Twins*, 61–69.

45. Twain, "On the Decay of the Art of Lying," in *CTSSE*, 1:828.

46. Forrester, *Truth Games*, 69, 74, 79. Forrester cites Freud's 1897 letter to Fleiss in which he observes that "there are no indications of reality in the unconscious, so that one cannot distinguish between truth and fiction that has been cathected with affect" (*Complete Letters of Freud to Fleiss*, 264). See also "Formulations on the Two Principles of Mental Functioning," in *SE*, 12:225.

47. Twain, "On the Decay of the Art of Lying," in *CTSSE*, 1:828–29.

48. See James Hopkins, "The Interpretation of Dreams," in *The Cambridge Companion to Freud*, ed. Jerome Neu (New York: Cambridge University Press, 1991), 87.

49. Quoted in *New York American*, May 26, 1907, in *Mark Twain: Life as I Find It*, ed. Charles Neider (Garden City, NY: Hanover House, 1961), 346.

50. *Mark Twain's Autobiography*, ed. Albert Bigelow Paine, 2 vols. (New York: Harper and Brothers, 1912), 2:246, 1:237. Twain was not exaggerating. His biographer, Albert Bigelow Paine, records that his subject's "marvelous reminiscences bore only an atmospheric relation to history" (*Mark Twain: A Biography*, 4 vols. [New York: Harper and Row, 1912], 4:1268).

51. Freud, *Civilization and Its Discontents*, in *SE*, 21:97.

52. Gay, *Freud*, 129.

53. Sigmund Freud, "Instincts and Their Vicissitudes," in *SE*, 14:120–21.

54. Sigmund Freud, *Beyond the Pleasure Principle*, in *SE*, 18:62. Freud's "entire model of pleasure," notes Sédat, which was "aimed at the relief of unpleasure, that is, of internal tensions and excitations that must be soothed, is one of organ pleasure produced by the discharge of tension" (*Freud*, 81). For an early version of the sexual model, see Freud's June 6, 1894, letter to Fleiss (*Complete Letters of Freud to Fleiss*, 79–80).

55. Kaja Silverman, *The Subject of Semiotics* (New York: Oxford University Press, 1983), 57.

56. *Beyond the Pleasure Principle*, in *SE*, 18:7. I have borrowed the military figure from Peter Gay (*Freud*, 337).

57. "What Is Man?" in *What Is Man? and Other Philosophical Writings*, ed. Paul Baender, 141, 145.

58. *Beyond the Pleasure Principle*, in *SE*, 18:7. The gloss on "mental events" derives from a note by Gregory Zilboorg on p. 111 of the Bantam edition, published in New York in 1959.

59. For a much fuller treatment, see my essay "Patterns of Consciousness in *The Innocents Abroad*," *American Literature* 58 (1986): 46–63. Roger B. Salomon's very apposite perspective appears in his book *Twain and the Image of History*, 205.

60. I am indebted for this broad overview to Kaja Silverman, *The Subject of Semiotics*, 60–61.

61. I hasten to qualify this general position. In doing so, I bow to the forceful words of Laplanche and Pontalis: "The idea of the pleasure principle undergoes little modification throughout Freud's work. What is problematic for him . . . is the position of this principle in its relation to other theoretical points of reference" (*The Language of Psychoanalysis*, 323). Not all stimulation originates internally. Freud says little about external sources, but notes in passing that their management is easily accomplished and soon becomes "a hereditary disposition." Instinctual stimuli are much more challenging, in good part because they "maintain an incessant and unavoidable afflux of stimulation" ("Instincts and Their Vicissitudes," *SE* 14:120). Nor are all instincts sexual. In his early work, Freud, ever the dualist, draws a distinction between ego drives (or instincts) concerned with self-preservation and sexual drives (or instincts) given over to erotic gratification and species survival. But the special authority of the sexual instincts is nonetheless conspicuous, both—as we have seen—as Freud's model for the behavior of the pleasure principle and as the leading source of the stimuli that trigger its

operations. Moreover, Freud emphasizes that the ego instincts are readily brought under the sway of the reality principle, with its sober regimen of moderation and deferral. By sharp contrast, the sexual instincts are incorrigibly resistant to discipline (*Introductory Lectures on Psychoanalysis, SE* 16:356–57). Not surprisingly, therefore, they are integral to Freud's discussions of the pleasure principle. In this light, I trust that my emphasis on the central importance of sexuality in Freud's conception of the pleasure principle will seem reasonable. I will turn to Freud's later distinction between the life instincts and the death instincts, Eros and Thanatos, in due course.

62. Twain, *What Is Man?* 486–87. "Buoyant spirits, comfort of mind, freedom from care—these happinesses we all have, at intervals; but in the spaces between, dear me, the black hours!" (*Christian Science*, in *What Is Man?* 349).

63. Paine, *Mark Twain: A Biography*, 1:65.

64. Mark Twain, *A Tramp Abroad*, The Oxford Mark Twain (New York: Oxford University Press, 1996), 126.

65. Samuel Clemens to Joseph Twichell, in *Mark Twain's Letters*, ed. Albert Bigelow Paine, 2 vols. (New York: Harper and Brothers, 1917), 2:558.

66. Mark Twain, "Down the Rhone," *Europe and Elsewhere*, in *The Writings of Mark Twain*, def. ed. (New York: Harper and Brothers, 1922–1925), 29:129, 139.

67. For details, see my "Patterns of Consciousness in *The Innocents Abroad*."

68. Sigmund Freud, "A Metapsychological Supplement to the Theory of Dreams," in *SE,* 14:222.

69. Freud, *Introductory Lectures on Psychoanalysis*, in *SE,* 15:88. See also *Introductory Lectures on Psychoanalysis*, in *SE,* 16:417.

70. Mark Twain, *The Innocents Abroad*, The Oxford Mark Twain (New York: Oxford University Press, 1996), 201.

71. Mark Twain, Speech at the New York Postgraduate School and Hospital Dinner, Jan. 20, 1908, MTP.

72. Mark Twain, "The Five Boons of Life," in *CTSSE*, 2:526.

73. Mark Twain, "Letters from the Earth," in *What Is Man?* 442–43.

74. Freud, *Civilization and Its Discontents*, in *SE*, 21:76.

75. Freud, *Beyond the Pleasure Principle*, in *SE,* 18:22, 29.

76. Ibid., 55–56, 38.

77. Adam Phillips, *Terrors and Experts* (Cambridge: Harvard University Press, 1996), 13–14.

78. Freud, "On the History of the Psycho-Analytic Movement," in *SE*, 14:16.

79. Sigmund Freud, "Repression," in *SE*, 14:147.

80. Clara Clemens, *My Father, Mark Twain* (New York: Harper and Brothers, 1931), 6–7.

81. Twain, *What Is Man?* 136, 469, 472–75.

82. Freud, *The Interpretation of Dreams*, in *SE*, 4:118–19, 160. This is of course the modified dream definition; the original, briefer version—"a dream is the fulfilment of a wish"—appears on ibid., 121. I take support for my reading of the Irma dream from much more detailed treatments by Hopkins, "The Interpretation of Dreams," 99–115, and Gay, *Freud*, 80–87.

83. Freud, *The Interpretation of Dreams*, in *SE*, 5:396.

84. James Hopkins observes that Freud "did not at this time give sufficient attention to the role of guilt" ("The Interpretation of Dreams," 130n26).

85. Freud, *The Interpretation of Dreams*, in *SE*, 4:113.

86. Peter Gay argues persuasively (*Freud*, 84–87) that the Irma dream was influenced by Freud's complex involvement, just a few months earlier, in his friend Fleiss's "disastrous" medical intervention with Emma Eckstein. In both cases, Freud's professional competence was centrally at issue; and in both he strained rather implausibly to displace responsibility onto others. Here, then, is guilt and its denial. An unconscious erotic motive is also crucially at play, Gay argues, in Freud's repressed homosexual feelings for Fleiss.

87. Paine, *Mark Twain: A Biography*, 4:1300.

88. Such is the argument of my book *The Author-Cat: Clemens's Life in Fiction* (New York: Fordham University, 2007).

89. William Dean Howells, "My Mark Twain," 277.

90. Samuel L. Clemens to Karl Gerhardt, May 1, 1883, MTP.

91. Dempsey, *Searching for Jim*, 279–80.

92. Guy Cardwell, *The Man Who Was Mark Twain* (New Haven: Yale University Press, 1991), 137.

93. Kaplan, *Mr. Clemens and Mark Twain*, 96.

94. Twain, "My Platonic Sweetheart," 35–36, MTP.

95. See Kaplan, *Mr. Clemens and Mark Twain*, 341–42; Arthur Pettit, *Mark Twain and the South* (Lexington: University Press of Kentucky, 1974), 150; and Cardwell, *The Man Who Was Mark Twain*, 134–36.

96. Freud to Fleiss, in *Complete Letters of Freud to Fleiss*, 272.

97. Sigmund Freud, *The Ego and the Id*, in *SE*, 19:34–35.

98. Ibid., 54. On Twain's melancholia, see my "Why I Killed My Brother: An Essay on Mark Twain," *Literature and Psychology* 30 (1980): 168–81.

99. Samuel Clemens to Mollie Stotts Clemens, June 18, 1858, MTP.

100. Sigmund Freud, *Totem and Taboo*, in *SE*, 13:145.

101. Freud, *Civilization and Its Discontents*, in *SE*, 21:123.

102. Freud, "Criminals from a Sense of Guilt," in *SE*, 14:332.

103. Gay, *Freud*, 487. For Freud's detailed discussions of anxiety, see *Inhibitions, Symptoms and Anxiety* and Lecture XXXII, "Anxiety and Instinctual Life," in *New Introductory Lectures on Psychoanalysis*, in *SE*, 22:81–111.

104. Sigmund Freud, "Some Character-Types Met with in Psychoanalytic Work," in *SE*, 14:329, 330,

105. Ibid., 332.

106. For much fuller treatments, see my essay "The Silences in *Huckleberry Finn*," *Nineteenth Century Fiction* 39 (1984): 1–23, and subsequent redactions in *In Bad Faith: The Dynamics of Deception in Mark Twain's America* (Cambridge: Harvard University Press, 1986) and *The Author-Cat: Clemens's Life in Fiction*.

107. Twain, "My First Lie and How I Got Out of It," in *CTSSE*, 2:439–41.

108. I have covered this ground before, and in more detail, most recently in *The Author-Cat*, 16–26.

109. Phillip Rieff, *Freud, The Mind of the Moralist* (New York: Viking, 1959), 277.

110. Jonathan Lear, *Freud* (New York: Routledge, 2005), 5–6. For a much more fully developed treatment of the mechanisms of bad faith in Twain's life and work, see chapters 1–2 of *The Author-Cat*.

111. Gay, *Freud*, 125.

112. Freud, "Thoughts for the Times on War and Death," in *SE*, 14:284.

113. Freud, "Repression," in *SE*, 14:153.

114. Freud, *The Ego and the Id*, in *SE*, 19:27, 51–52. For more on the implications of Freud's argument, see Herbert Fingarette, *Self-Deception* (London: Routledge and Kegan Paul, 1969), 113–16.

115. Freud, *Civilization and Its Discontents*, in *SE*, 21:144.

116. Twain, "What Is Man?" in *What Is Man?* 481–82.

117. Twain, "The Character of Man," in *What Is Man?* 61. "Hypocrisy, envy, malice, cruelty, vengefulness, seduction, rape, robbery, swindling, arson, bigamy, adultery, and the oppression and humiliation of

the poor and the helpless in all ways, have been and still are more or less common among both the civilized and uncivilized peoples of the earth" ("Man's Place in the Animal World," in *What Is Man?* 80).

118. Freud, *Introductory Lectures on Psychoanalysis*, in *SE*, 15:146; *Civilization and Its Discontents*, in *SE*, 21:122.

119. Freud, *Civilization and Its Discontents*, in *SE*, 21:105, 122–24, 143.

120. Mark Twain, "The Secret History of Eddypus," in *Mark Twain's Fables of Man*, ed. John S. Tuckey (Berkeley: University of California Press, 1972), 327.

121. Freud, *Civilization and Its Discontents*, in *SE*, 21:134.

122. Isabel Lyon, Diary, September 23, 1905, MTP.

123. Mark Twain, "Eve's Diary," in *CTSSE*, 2:708. The essay was first published in *Harper's Monthly* in 1905.

124. Twain, "Letters from the Earth," in *CTSSE*, 2:884–85. Written in late 1909, just months before Twain's death, "Letters from the Earth" was not published until 1962.

125. Sigmund Freud, "'Civilized' Sexual Morality and Modern Nervous Illness," in *SE*, 9:191.

126. Freud, *Civilization and Its Discontents*, in *SE*, 21:132.

127. Cf. "Eve Speaks," in *CTSSE*, 2:710–12; and "Which Was It?" in *Which Was the Dream?* ed. Tuckey, 234–40.

128. Mark Twain, Notebook 35, MTP.

129. This, in very condensed form, is the argument of the chapter on *Huckleberry Finn* in my *In Bad Faith: The Dynamics of Deception in Mark Twain's America* (Cambridge: Harvard University Press, 1986). On *Pudd'nhead Wilson* as "unreadable," see Hershel Parker, *Flawed Texts and Verbal Icons: Literary Authority in American Fiction* (Evanston: Northwestern University Press, 1984).

130. Freud, "The Uncanny," in *SE*, 17:234, 235, 241, 237.

131. Twain, "Which Was It?" in *Which Was the Dream?* ed. Tuckey, 267, 415.

132. Freud, "The Uncanny," in *SE*, 17:241. For a much more fully elaborated treatment of "Which Was It?" see *The Author-Cat*, 195–99.

133. Twain, "Which Was It?" in *Which Was the Dream?* ed Tuckey, 406.

Three

TWAIN AND MARX

CATHERINE CARLSTROEM
AND FORREST G. ROBINSON

William Dean Howells once sagely observed that his famous friend Mark Twain was a theoretical socialist and a practical aristocrat (*MTHL* 2:579). Even as he objected in principle to greed and speculation, Twain was hopelessly addicted to a dream of vast personal wealth; even as he passionately defended American democracy, he was given to harangues against politicians, the ballot, and the judicial system; even as he reveled in American equality and despised aristocracy, he wanted nothing so much as to be a king. Ambivalence and contradiction pervaded his life and works. As a Southerner from a slave-owning family who had witnessed some of its worst abuses he condemned slavery, yet continued to be harried by a sense of moral complicity in the evils of the peculiar institution. Although he sometimes longed—like another nineteenth-century critic, Karl Marx—for revolution, his hunger for wealth, coupled with his powerful pessimism about human nature, ensured that however deeply he damned capitalism, he could neither believe in, nor commit to, its destruction.

During his brief residence in New York City between late August and late October, 1853, young Sam Clemens (who would not be eighteen until November) worked at a print shop and boarded nearby at a rooming house on Duane Street. During his spare time he visited the New York World's Fair, went to the theater, and spent evenings reading in the printers' free library. In his letters home, which were published in his brother Orion's newspaper, the *Hannibal Journal,* he reported on working conditions, the size and diversity of the city's population, and the splendors of the Crystal Palace. While this subject matter hints at his incipient interest in socioeconomic issues, he made no deep study of them. If he was keeping up with the news, then he may have perused one or more of Karl Marx's many articles—most reporting on and analyzing events in Europe—which were appearing at regular intervals in the *New York Daily Tribune.* Otherwise, there is little in the record to suggest that Twain and Marx were at all aware of each other. Marx took scant interest in humor of any kind, and Twain viewed communism with grave suspicion. Worlds apart and separated by almost a generation in years (Marx was born in 1818, Twain in 1835), they appear to have had almost nothing in common.

Yet in their distant and entirely separate realms, the two men shared many qualities and ideas, including similar critiques of the economic systems and practices of their societies, parallels that are especially surprising given their disparate personal relationships to capitalism. These cognate analyses were rooted, perhaps, in their deliberate gravitation to human experience in its common, everyday, concrete reality. Following Ludwig Feuerbach, who viewed God as a projection of a human ideal, Marx brought Hegelian idealism down to earth, insisting that the pursuit of airy abstractions such as Spirit, Mind, and the Absolute was antipodal to the real business of philosophy, which must begin with the finite, material world of actual men and women in their present condition. For his part, Twain would go on to become the voice of a new American vernacular tradition in literature. He would ridicule the romantic excesses of Scott and Cooper, and in his own writing he would supplant their gaudy heroes and heroines with ordinary people doing ordinary things in ordinary American places. Whether conceived as theoretical categories like workers and owners, or literary constructs like Huck Finn and Injun Joe, the material conditions of the commonplace people that the two authors observed demanded their attention.

They both found that the world lost none of its mystery when the focus descended from the lofty and refined to the everyday, and they both directed attention to things so very ordinary that they seemed inevitable, yet turned out, when closely observed, to make no sense at all. Economics provided countless examples: "A commodity," Marx reflects, may appear to be "a very trivial thing, and easily understood." But "analysis shows that it is, in reality, a very queer thing, abounding in metaphysical subtleties and theological niceties" (*MER* 319). Twain would make a similar discovery about commodities when he commenced writing about an unwashed, illiterate country boy and his companion, a runaway slave named Jim, taking flight downriver on a makeshift raft. Something as apparently straightforward and taken for granted as slavery, Huck Finn soon discovers, could turn out to defy all reckoning. The two authors' lives would be spent puzzling out, in print and in person, just such conundrums.

Marx was born in the German Rhineland town of Trier. His parents were liberal Jews of comfortable means who had converted to Protestantism in order to ease the way for his father's professional advancement. Marx's characteristic seriousness and rigor emerged when he became a dedicated student of philosophy, joined the Young Hegelian movement in Berlin, and completed his doctorate in 1841. Failing to land a university lectureship, he soon met Friedrich Engels, married Jenny von Westphalen, started a family, and settled into a career as a radical journalist with a special interest in political economy. His continuing studies in history, philosophy, and economics took written form in materials later published as "Economic and Philosophic Manuscripts of 1844." Here Marx set out the rudiments of an interpretation of history, revolution, and the future of communism that would occupy him as a leading radical theorist and political activist for the rest of his life. Drawing on what he describes as "a wholly empirical analysis based on the conscientious critical study of political economy," he concludes that the contemporary worker under capital has been reduced

> to the level of a commodity and becomes indeed the most wretched of commodities; that the wretchedness of the worker is in inverse proportion to the power and magnitude of his production; that the necessary result of competition is the accumulation of capital in a few hands, and thus the restoration of monopoly in a more terrible form; that finally the distinction between capitalist and land-rentier, like that between the tiller of the soil and the factory-worker, disappears and that the whole of society must fall apart into two classes—the property-*owners* and the propertyless *workers*. (*MER* 67, 70)

His developing ideas crystallized memorably four years later in the *Manifesto of the Communist Party*, which Marx, in collaboration with Engels, first published in London in 1848. Designed as a "theoretical and practical programme" for the Communist League, a secret international association of radical workers, the tract announces that "the spectre of Communism" is "haunting Europe," and that "the history of all hitherto existing society is the history of class struggles." The communist agenda is then presented: the violent overthrow of capital by the proletariat; the abolition of private property; and the supplanting of class distinctions with a socialist order "in which the free development of each is the condition for the free development of all" (*MER* 491).

By the time Marx was twenty-five, his major commitments in love and work had taken their final form. Thereafter his biography is the record of dedication to the people and the causes closest to him, and most especially to the analysis and public discussion of what was wrong with the world as he found it. As a man of great learning and gravitas Marx gave most of his waking hours to study, writing, intellectual conversation, and political organizing. His material needs were relatively modest and his pleasures were few.

By contrast, Mark Twain was as varied in his interests (as a businessman, journalist, novelist, and celebrity) and as volatile in his moods as the German was steadfast and stable. The American at twenty-five had little idea where his life would take him. True, he was very happily piloting steamboats on the Mississippi, but that would end with the outbreak of the Civil War. Though a Southern loyalist, he decided against getting shot at, and in 1861 he left for the gold and silver mines in California and Nevada. During the next decade he traveled widely in the United States and Europe, working as a miner, a speculator, a journalist, and a humorous lecturer, before settling down in his mid-thirties as a successful and very wealthy family man and popular travel writer, novelist, and public personality.

But even in his mature years Mark Twain was a protean personality, a loose federation of often contradictory selves, professions, affiliations, ideas, moods, and points of view. While, like Marx, Twain knew there was something very wrong with the world around him, he had none of Marx's acuity when it came to identifying and precisely defining what bothered him, and none of his unwavering dedication to amending it. Was the problem the fever of speculation that infected Americans after the war, the failure of liberal democratic institutions, the refusal of the South to reform and to rejoin the rest of the country, or the nation's fateful entry into the international race for imperial possessions? All these problems vied for his condemnation, but unlike Marx, he could create no grand theory, no master schema to incorporate, explain, and remedy them. Where Marx was characteristically direct and unambiguous, Twain was almost invariably driven by conflicting conscious and unconscious impulses into a posture of ambivalence visible in his life and works.

This sharp contrast between the two men is traceable to the striking difference in their sense of personal relationship to the problems that concerned them both. Marx viewed capital as a social and economic pathology for whose creation he felt no personal responsibility. His scorn for the bourgeoisie was apparently unmingled with any complicating sense of involvement in their lives and enterprises. For Twain, things could not have been more

different. His desire to achieve the social standing whose foundations he reviled as unconscionable led to hypocrisy in his life and
marked inconsistencies in his works, most notably in the equal
measures of scorn and reverence for wealth and power that he
poured into *A Connecticut Yankee in King Arthur's Court.* Where
Marx laid claim to scientific objectivity in his analysis and critique, Twain retreated in bad-faith denial from the acknowledgment of his entanglement in the grave problems against which
he leveled his attack. Marx the philosopher was focused, systematic, and coolly objective in his analysis of the mysteries of capital. By contrast, Twain the essayist, travel writer, and novelist was
so variously implicated in the problems he surveyed that he was
seldom capable of achieving, let alone sustaining, a detached perspective on them. As a result, his criticism was frequently shad-
owed by intimations of personal guilt nowhere to be found in
Marx's writing. In their address to very similar problems, then,
Marx knew exactly where he stood, while Twain often failed to
recognize that he was rather squarely positioned in his own line
of fire.[1]

   In spite of the sharp differences in their approaches, our protagonists' personal and intellectual lives featured prominent similarities. Some may simply be amusing superficialities—having
lawyer fathers, loving cigars, being challenged to duels—while
others—their careers as journalists and their respective economic circumstances, for example—informed their work in both
subtle and obvious ways. Both came from families whose real if
modest social pretensions were hampered by their fathers' pre-
mature deaths. Marx's and Twain's reduced circumstances im-
proved as each author married into wealth, but both continued
to rely heavily on income from in-laws, were unsuccessful money managers, and frequently overspent their means. Their ambiguous class standing and uncertain finances may have attuned
them early on to problems in their societies' social, political, and
economic systems. Susceptible to anger and capable of eloquent
indignation, both became versatile prose stylists who wrote critically, often passionately, and at length about these systems, and
lent their considerable weight to major political causes.[2]

Marx, as we have observed, is everywhere witness to and critical of a world divided between the bourgeoisie, an elite, proper-
ty-owning class who control the means of production, and the
proletariat, the much larger class of property-less but ostensibly
"free" workers who are oppressed and immiserated by the conditions of life under capital. Any reader of *A Connecticut Yankee
in King Arthur's Court* will know that Twain recognized and deplored the same division between the powerful and the weak, the
rich and the poor. Nor, it should be added, was this a condition
unique, in his assessment, to the medieval period in which the
novel is set. In "The New Dynasty," a speech delivered at the Hartford Monday Evening Club in 1886 (at about the same time that
he commenced work on *A Connecticut Yankee*), Twain turned
to the question, "Who are the oppressors?" They are "the few,"
he replied: "the king, the capitalist, and a handful of other over-
seers and superintendents. Who the oppressed? The many: The
nations of the earth; the valuable personages; the workers; they
that MAKE the bread that the soft-handed and the idle eat. Why is
it right that there is not a fairer division of the spoil all around?
BECAUSE LAWS AND CONSTITUTIONS HAVE ORDERED OTHERWISE"
(*CTSSE* 1:884).

Twain is here similar to Marx, both in characterizing the op-
pressor/oppressed relation as an *international* phenomenon ("the
nations of the earth") and in insisting that capitalist hegemony
thrives on the collaborative support of the state. On this latter
point, Marx is emphatic in the *Manifesto of the Communist Party* that "the bourgeoisie has . . . conquered for itself in the modern representative State, exclusive political sway. The executive of
the modern State is but a committee for managing the common
affairs of the whole bourgeoisie" (*MER* 475). Twain is also like
Marx in the boldness with which he speaks truth to power. The
Hartford Monday Evening Club, as Jerome Loving describes it,
was a "citadel of insurance brokers and investment bankers,"[3] the
very oppressors whom Twain condemns in his speech. Quite unlike Marx, however, Twain was himself a leading member of the
elite capitalist class that he singled out for criticism. Indeed, we
may suppose that his status as a wealthy entrepreneur afforded

him a kind of license to voice his disapproval with such striking candor in their midst. After all, no one in that room could have failed to recognize that the speaker's condemnation was *self-condemnation* at the same time. *A Connecticut Yankee* invites interpretation as a fictional dramatization of this largely unconscious tension, and of the repressed guilt that went with it.

Marx and Twain were aligned in drawing a sharp distinction between free human productivity on one side and grinding toil on the other. The theory of historical materialism is summed up in Marx's familiar declaration from *A Contribution to the Critique of Political Economy*, "It is not the consciousness of men that determines their being, but, on the contrary, their social being that determines their consciousness" (*MER* 4). Twain offers his own variation on this theme, noting what Marx might identify as the effects of ideology, in "Corn-Pone Opinions," an essay written in 1901 in which a black preacher takes as his text the statement, "You tell me whar a man gits his corn-pone, en I'll tell you what his 'pinions is." Here he echoes the observation that people's "social being," including the influence of owners, of bosses, of the structure of the economic system one labors within, exerts great force on their thought. People's consciousnesses, like their bodies, are built from material forces, their "'pinions" effortlessly ingested along with their food. Twain explains: "Broadly speaking, there are none but corn-pone opinions. . . . I think that in the majority of cases [they] are unconscious and not calculated; that [they are] born of the human being's natural yearning to stand well with his fellows, and have their inspiring approval and praise" (*CTSSE* 2:507, 510). Community support, then, is here also yoked to the economic status quo.

Religion was another leading influence on the formation of consciousness that both Marx and Twain identified, and both saw it as a potent force for ill. Like the economic systems they critiqued, religion rests in and is upheld by myth and illusion, and they noted how the two forces often converged to maintain systems of privilege and power. Following Feuerbach, Marx regarded religion as a prime expression of alienation, a construction detached from its social origins and experienced in human life as a mysterious and powerful outside force. As he put it, "*Man makes religion*, religion does not make man." In his "Contribution to the Critique of Hegel's *Philosophy of Right*," Marx called for the abolition of religion because he aimed to free people from the "opium" of illusory happiness in order to prepare them for the much richer satisfactions of the truth (*MER* 53–54). Twain certainly agreed that religious belief was the offspring of entirely illusory human fabrications. Toward the end of *No. 44, The Mysterious Stranger*, he dismisses the rudiments of Christianity as "pure and puerile insanities, the silly creations of an imagination that is not conscious of its freaks—in a word, they are a dream" (*MS* 405). Both abhorred how religious doctrine, however illusory, was readily and successfully employed to support nefarious ends, whether under feudalism, capitalism, or imperialism. Twain dramatized this in numerous works, perhaps most overtly in *A Connecticut Yankee*, in "To the Person Sitting in Darkness," and in describing La Salle's taking of Native-owned lands in *Life on the Mississippi*.

But as a man afflicted with a predatory conscience, Twain acknowledged—albeit rather grudgingly—that illusions could afford precious solace to sore minds. Religion is a dream, but it has real effects, positive and negative, abstract and material. Thus he scorned Mary Baker Eddy as a shameless fraud and hypocrite, but conceded nonetheless that her religion freed many of its adherents from the torments of guilt and depression. "The vacuous vulgarity" of Eddy's writings "was a perpetual joy to him," Howells shrewdly observes, "while he bowed with serious respect to the sagacity which built so securely upon the everlasting rock of human credulity and folly."[4] He was also greatly impressed by the wealth she amassed through her religious empire, a fortune built like his, by fictions, hers designed to console, his as likely to disturb as to reassure. Once again, then, Marx and Twain substantially agree on a major issue, parting ways only—but quite predictably—when the pressure of conscience makes itself felt in Twain's developing reflections.

Our subjects surveyed the world with moral outrage and at the same time rejected conventional morality. As Robert C. Tucker observes, "*Capital* was written by an angry man" who was obviously moved by a spirit of "moral condemnation and protest" (*MER* xxxi). Yet Marx was also scornfully dismissive of the ideologically driven moral pretensions of the bourgeoisie.[5] For his part, Twain unleashed righteous rage at the spectacle of pervasive injustice and folly, but at intervals of sustained philosophical reflection—and in manner reminiscent of Marx—he heaped contempt on what he called "that mongrel Moral Sense. . . . A Sense whose function is to distinguish between right and wrong, with liberty to choose," almost always incorrectly, between them. Twain's famous description of *Huckleberry Finn* as a collision between "a sound heart and a deformed conscience"[6] highlights the distinction both the American and the German make between the socially constructed, religion-mediated conscience and some sort of undefined yet fundamental, a priori morality based in material reality and rational truth.

While Marx was comfortable making ethical propositions without recourse to religion, Twain could not keep the two sufficiently distinct, and guilt was a crushing consequence. In good part because it fostered guilt, Twain warmed to the idea of doing completely without morality. "There shouldn't *be* any wrong," he argues, "and without the Moral Sense there *couldn't* be any" (*MS* 72–73). Huck Finn puts the case even more memorably, allowing that "whether you do right or wrong, a person's conscience ain't got no sense, and just goes for him *anyway*. If I had a yaller dog that didn't know no more than a person's conscience does, I would pison him" (*HF* 290). Huck voices Twain's belief that there is a right and a wrong by showing how religious dogma about slavery has reversed them, as well as his creator's certainty that he will suffer regardless of his choice. This dooms the moral enterprise even while proclaiming it necessary. Given the inadequacy of the Moral Sense, the ensuing guilt regardless of the choice, how are people to know if they have thrown off illusion or embraced it?

For Marx, rationality and discipline would suffice. In his audaciously titled work "For a Ruthless Criticism of Everything Existing," the youthful Marx trained his sights on "the reform of consciousness" which "consists *only* in enabling the world to clarify its consciousness, in waking it from its dream about itself. . . . Our whole task can consist only in putting religious and political questions into self-conscious human form" (*MER* 15). Marx was confident not only that he could identify illusions when he saw them, but also that he had discovered the way to live entirely without them. "The call [to humans] to abandon their illusions about their condition," he boldly declared in "Contribution to Hegel's *Philosophy of Right*," "is a *call to abandon a condition which requires illusions*" (*MER* 54). Twain was in complete agreement on the first point. Young Satan, who speaks for him in *The Mysterious Stranger*, "was accustomed to say that our race lived a life of continuous and uninterrupted self-deception. It duped itself from cradle to grave with shams and delusions which it mistook for realities, and this made its entire life a sham" (*MS* 164). He was less sanguine, however, about a cure. In *A Connecticut Yankee*, Hank Morgan lays plans for the awakening of sixth-century England into the clear light of nineteenth-century reality. He aims to free the multitudes from the lies and delusions that are exploited by the state and the religious establishment to produce a nation of slaves, both the kind that "wore the iron collar on their necks," and all the rest as well, who "were slaves in fact, but without the name." Such people, Hank observes ironically, "imagined themselves men and freemen, and called themselves so" (*CY* 98). But rationality fails. His revolution fizzles badly and then backfires completely, largely because his assumptions about history prove to be unfounded. The most important illusion of all, he learns to his dismay, is *his* illusion about progress.

All of which brings us to the matter of human nature. Twain is of course well known for his angry denunciations of "the damned human race."[7] Humans in Twain's reckoning are by nature perverse. Driven by the forces of character, training, and circumstance, we are doomed to the repetition over time of hapless surrenders to greed, cruelty, violence, and self-deception. Flawed structures and behavior can be critiqued and reforms proposed, but the innate defects that produce individual immorality and exploitative systems are fixed, ineradicable, and therefore insuperable obstacles to permanent change. This is the emergent thrust of *A Connecticut Yankee*, a novel whose principal theme, according to Roger B. Salomon, "is the absurdity of optimism and the impermanence of progress (or the illusory nature of progress) because of the aggressiveness and rapacity of modern industrial man, the false promise of technology and—ultimately—because of the deep-rootedness of human evil."[8]

Marx was similarly suspicious of industrial capitalism and the alleged benefits of technology, but much more upbeat about human nature and the prospects for historical change, believing that although humans are by nature creative and free, their consciousness under capital is unable to grasp the contradictions and irrationalities of their social circumstances. Marx was nonetheless confident that those circumstances, though they act coercively on individuals in the present, are mutable and therefore subject to changes that would lead inevitably to the liberation of human creativity once communist society had been achieved. In the course of this ineluctable historical march toward the ultimate "realm of freedom," he assumed that humans would respond constructively to the tasks that changing material conditions presented to them. Quite unlike Twain, then, Marx argues that historical change is both inevitable and progressive. Hence his confident declaration in "Theses on Feuerbach" that while "the philosophers have only *interpreted* the world," his own ultimate objective "is to change it" (*MER* 145).[9]

Neither being favorably disposed to nineteenth-century civilization, both writers saw plenty in need of change. While other writers and activists also called for various reforms of the period's excesses, Twain and Marx focused much of their attention on the same targets, decrying their age as the apogee of industrial capitalism, a potent collaboration between the state and the bourgeoisie in which an elite minority of the wealthy exploited the vast majority of workers, all the while persuading them that their debased condition was necessary and even desirable. Seeking to reveal this relation, they turned their gaze outward, for while capital could partially conceal its predatory intentions at home, the mask came off abroad, revealing the true ferocity of civilization. As Marx pronounces in his essay "The Future Results of British Rule in India," published in the *New York Daily Tribune* on August 8, 1853, "The profound hypocrisy and inherent barbarism of bourgeois civilization lies unveiled before our eyes, turning from its home, where it assumes respectable forms, to the colonies, where it goes naked" (*MER* 663). Twain takes an identical tack in "To the Person Sitting in Darkness," published in 1901, where he observes that the civilized world thinks of itself as the benign agent of freedom, equality, justice, and Christian charity. But this is a happy illusion reserved "for Home Consumption." In fact, the putative beneficiaries of civilization pay for its "blessings" with their "blood and tears and land and liberty" (*CTSSE* 2:461–62).

Moving beyond suggestions of their numerous and close affinities, we will now lay out key elements of Marx's thought as a reference for the ensuing discussion of rich parallels in Twain's work. Marx takes a ground–up, rather than a head–down, approach to reality. He begins not with ideas, but with labor, free productive activity, which is at once the essence of human life and the main driver of history.[10] When, in the latest stage of human social evolution under capitalism, workers' productive activity is channeled into labor over which humans appear to have no control, they are alienated from their essential humanity. Such alienation has multiple dimensions. Most fundamentally, labor is alienated from its products, which have become commodities, things produced not for their direct use, but for exchange. Like religions, Marx argues, commodities are social constructions that have achieved an illusory objectivity and independence. When we forget that we are their creators, we make fetishes of commodities by conferring upon them greater autonomy and authority than they actually possess. Like religious idols, commodities may thus assume an unnatural mastery over their creators. Marx's principal aim in his masterpiece, *Capital*, is to penetrate the superficial logic of capitalism, and thereby to reveal to workers their unconscious subjection to the deeper economic forces that they in fact created and over which they should assume conscious authority. In short, he summons the proletariat to a journey from alienation to freedom.

Under capitalism, Marx argues, members of the proletariat sell their labor to capitalists, who in turn use their profit (the surplus value left over after workers' minimal needs are met) to accumulate more wealth. But as capitalists expand their assets, workers are reduced to conditions of intolerable degradation. Wages fall; smaller capitalists are forced out of business and into an expanding labor force; thanks to technological innovation, work becomes more grindingly repetitive and monotonous; overproduction fosters ever sharper economic crises. Such conditions, Marx insists, are not natural, as classical economists suggest; rather, they are pathologies unique to the socially created capitalist order.

Because they have lost control of the productive process, laborers are also alienated from one another, believing as they do that selfishness and competition are integral to their human nature. Their error in this regard illustrates Marx's view that the economic structure of society ("the relations of production") drives consciousness, and not the other way around. That same economic structure informs the multiple dimensions—religious, legal, political, esthetic—of experience under capitalism that combine to win worker acquiescence in the unnatural degradation of their lives. Seduced by what Engels called "false consciousness," members of the proletariat are hopelessly alienated from the grave reality of their actual condition. They imagine themselves free when in fact they are slaves to a system of exploitation which they neither understand nor control.

In primitive societies, Marx observes, people work very hard to meet basic needs, but they are spared the dire consequences of alienation because property is held in common. How then, he asks, did capitalists amass sufficient wealth to set the new order in motion? He concludes that it must have resulted from a period of "primitive accumulation . . . preceding capitalistic accumulation," an historical development that "plays in Political Economy about the same part as original sin in theology," and in which "conquest, enslavement, robbery, murder, briefly force, play the great part" (*MER* 431–32). In the sequel to primitive accumulation, two distinct classes emerge: a small elite who take private ownership of property and control the means of production, and a mass of laborers who, in passing over time from feudal economic conditions to those of industrial capitalism, are reduced to servitude as wage workers without alternative means of subsistence. Such, in Marx's reckoning, is the historical background to the multiform alienation of the modern proletariat.

The solution to the problem is in the dialectical resolution of all forms of alienation that will come with the revolutionary rise of the proletariat and the subsequent advent of communism, which, with the abolition of private property, will yield a final synthesis in which humans are at last free to be their true selves and to appreciate the world without need of possessing it. This is the final goal toward which history tends. Clearly, Marx believed that revolution was necessary and inevitable, and that members of the proletariat would engage actively in bringing it about.

Marx's conviction contrasts starkly with Twain's skepticism that a solution to these both existential and economic dilemmas was even possible. Twain's reformer's zeal ran headlong into his entrenched cynicism about human nature and the limits it imposes on socio-political progress. Our writers' disparate visions of the unfolding of human history, of the tractability of economic ills, necessarily depended on their differing beliefs about the origins of those ills and on their understandings of human nature. Twain positions the problem of economic injustice deeper than Marx, in the human nature that was both author of and subject to its institutions. Where Marx posits economic exploitation as an outcome of social forms, of specific practices, of particular financial instruments (e.g., private property, capital accumulation), Twain pushes his origination story back further, into the human psyche, which he declares to be infected with greed and selfishness. The processes that Marx identifies as alienation appear in Twain, but linked to a different origin myth, the biblical story of original sin, which explains our nature and its consequences. In Twain, the variety of human-economic ills—land-grabbing, slavery, colonialism, imperialism, capitalism, as well as the constant robberies perpetrated by individuals—are merely branches of a tree rooted in the cursed and intractable human condition. These selfish impulses toward self-interest will never be "enlightened" in Adam Smith's sense and turned to the advancement of society.

Marx's optimism reflected a nexus of related beliefs: that external structures—material conditions—shape people's consciousness, creating ideologies that may retard progress, but also that unjust systems are condemned to revolutionary change by their own self-destructive natures. Capitalism inevitably will bring about its own fall. Ideologies collapse as people come to understand the true conditions of their social lives. Richard W. Miller argues that Marx's working definition of ideology affords the hope that different social beliefs may promote change, that "just as there are truth-distorting social forces, there are [also] truth-promoting ones."[11] Thus human consciousness will change in the course of the transformation of the economic system, and in its new form will contribute to and hasten the revolution. His optimism is nowhere more visible than when he assures us that we are destined to this progress because "mankind always sets itself only such tasks as it can solve; since, looking at the matter more closely, it will always be found that the task arises only when the material conditions for its solution already exist or are at least in the process of formation" (*MER* 5). Because human consciousness evolves with its economic systems, solutions emerge as problems are recognized.

Twain agrees that much of human consciousness, including individual conscience, is largely determined by culture, and in turn by the ruling class. This is why Huck Finn is certain that he will go to hell for freeing Jim, and why Twain's mother, Jane, accepted slavery without question in spite of being a pious Christian; it is why Hank Morgan thinks that advertising and free trade will amend the scourge of feudalism. However, while Marx believed that entrenched *systems* of oppression were most responsible for tyranny and could be eradicated, Twain, while in agreement about the injustices, cruelties, and senselessness of these systems, assigned the blame to their creators. The same human nature that formed and upheld these systems could partially or temporarily change or even abolish them, but ultimately the impetus—impulses of greed, the drives for status and power— would reassert itself. Selfishness, though practiced on a massive scale only by the dominant classes, is nevertheless every human's birthright. False-consciousness of one kind will be succeeded by another. This is not, however, absolute; we are also innately capable of goodness.

Twain characterizes American culture as profoundly and pervasively conflicted. His characters frequently have instinctive and undeveloped desires for equality and fairness that transcend cultural forces, and they experience moments when the arbitrariness of privilege is manifest to them and, in some cases, disturbs or rankles. Huck feels rather than thinks that Jim deserves freedom; Roxy complains to the privileged infant whom she nurses alongside her own baby, "What has my po' baby done, dat he couldn't have yo' luck? He hain't done nuth'n" (*PW* 14). In spite of such promising trends, however, Twain's characters' inchoate sense of justice is no match for natural selfishness or ingrained ideology. They long less for equality than for distinction. The powerful wish to retain privilege, the unfortunate to attain it. Even relatively enlightened and sympathetic ostensible heroes—Huck Finn, Pudd'nhead Wilson, Hank Morgan—retreat from obligations to equality and justice when they begin to realize the personal and social costs entailed by such enlightened commitments.

Marx viewed people as far more willing to cede privilege and power, reading their desire for it as driven by external, structural forces. According to Terence Ball, Marx believed that where capitalists may resist a fall from power, members of the proletariat will be more accepting: "Once the workers consolidated their power and the threat of counterrevolution receded, the coercive interim state that Marx called the dictatorship of the proletariat would lose its reason for existing and could therefore be expected to 'wither away.'"[12] For Twain, power confers on its holders its own reason for existing. Though consonant with Marx in believing that society fosters immorality in its individual members,

Twain also saw the human conscience as so easily confounded by its own bad-faith rationalizations of wrongdoing that it reinforces the corrupting influences at play in its social environment or constructs new modes of subjugation. While Marx imagined the work of revolution as progressive, for Twain reform is eternally, infernally recursive, a job that can never be finished.

Twain witnessed firsthand the failures of Reconstruction, and everywhere observed that oppressive structures endure unchanged through the vicissitudes of various systems and role-players. This important point is illustrated in several major texts: The oppressive Hawaiian royalty gives way to the tyranny of white Christian missionaries in *Roughing It*. At the end of *Huckleberry Finn*, in his grand "evasion" scheme, Tom knows that Jim has been manumitted, but withholds this saving information, exposing his friend to genuine dangers, privations, and cruelties, all in order to prolong the fun of playing at freeing an already free man. His thoughtless manipulation serves as a reminder of the fate of all freed blacks in post-Reconstruction America, when de jure slavery gave way to the de facto oppressions of sharecropping, segregation, imprisonment under the black codes, and an epidemic of lynching. In *A Connecticut Yankee*, the feudalism of sixth-century England will, in spite of Hank's attempts to engender an age of enlightenment, inevitably lead back to the same nineteenth century he has left, its legacies of slavery and its penchant for racist imperialism cheek by jowl with its promises of unprejudiced meritocracy, and its industrial efficiency best symbolized by Hank's employer there, the bustling, profitable arms factory, cheerfully churning out the tools of conquest, coercion, and murder. *Pudd'nhead Wilson's* heroine, Roxy, manages to subvert her oppressors by switching her slave child for her master's child, thereby enslaving one innocent infant to free another. Roxy swiftly re-creates the very damaging hierarchy whose rationale she has just exposed as false and arbitrary, becoming "the dupe of her own deceptions" (*PW* 20), in thrall now to a new but equally powerful and homicidal master, her own son, who is no less a fake, yet no less real, than the master whose place he has taken. It is indeed the system that corrupts her, as Marx would have observed, but she is the knowing architect of her own continued enslavement within it. While *Life on the Mississippi* dramatizes La Salle's appropriation of lands and people under the "confiscation cross" at the mouth of the Mississippi River, Twain depicts the shadow of the cross, of religiously justified theft, extended internationally in his later, anti-imperialist writings. With excruciating irony, "To the Person Sitting in Darkness" details the harnessing of American ideals of freedom and equality to the arrogant barbarism of manifest destiny and empire.

For human progress to stick, both individuals and societies must permanently renounce selfish instincts. Given his assumptions about human nature, Twain knew that such reform would always fail. Yet he persisted nonetheless in exposing and condemning our moral lapses, as if to suggest that the inevitability of failure in no way releases us from the obligation to continue to resist greed and injustice. In light of his pessimism, Twain's gravitation to philosophical determinism is less remarkable than his dogged, acute critiques and the ongoing, vigorous calls for reform that punctuated most of his career. Unfazed by the glaring contradiction in his thinking, Twain continued to condemn poverty, violence, and injustice even as he continued to believe that they were intractable evils for which human beings would likely accept no ultimate responsibility.

The contradiction was of course a sure-fire recipe for guilt arising out of the unavoidable human failure to match deeds with untenable moral aspirations. Guilt in turn fuels a predilection for self-justification, which, toward the very end of his career, in the solipsistic *No. 44, The Mysterious Stranger*, published posthumously, Twain insists is "the way we are made" (*MS* 348). Seduced by the Moral Sense into the groundless illusion of their own goodness, humans retreat from the guilty awareness of their transgressions into varieties of bad-faith denial. Chief among such evasive strategies is the recurrent claim that we are in bondage to the necessity of our nature and therefore free from responsibility for our iniquity. "The several temperaments constitute a law of God, a command of God," Twain insists, and "whatsoever is done in obedience to that law is blameless."[13] Thus even as he deplored injustice and publicly denounced slavery and imperialism, his experience of life and the intolerable burden of personal guilt strongly inclined him to the moral consolations of determinism.

In counterweight, Twain knew all too well that rationalization provides an easier way than righteousness to assuage the demands of an exacting and unsatisfied conscience. He observes in *No. 44, The Mysterious Stranger* that "when we want a thing badly we go hunting for good and righteous reasons for it; we give it a fine name to comfort our consciences, whereas we privately know we are only hunting for plausible ones" (348). The book both exposes and illustrates this evasive tactic; it ends with the protagonist's realization that the world is unreal, and that he is but a transient thought, liberated from life's troubles and demands, and immune to the tricks of a deranged moral imagination. Twain would seem, then, to give over fully to this concluding nihilism; but his novel's acute analysis of our dismissal of recognized ethical responsibilities draws attention to the familiar and enduring tension in his ideas.

Twain's impulse to disregard the world, with all its impossible moral demands, reflects what T. J. Jackson Lears, in *No Place of Grace,* sees as a leading feature of the zeitgeist of his age, which had witnessed not only the disintegration of the moral authorities, both religious and secular, that had upheld slavery, but also a rapidly changing, industrializing economy that was further destabilizing human relations and obligations. Lears observes that "the process of secularization exacerbated the problem of personal responsibility, and contributed significantly to the sense of unreality underlying the crisis of cultural authority." Marx, he points out, directly commented in the *Manifesto of the Communist Party* on the disorientation that accompanies industrialization, "in which the inner dynamic of capitalism dissolves all stable social relations and settled convictions: 'All that is solid melts into air, all that is holy is profane.'"[14] Rather than face what he recognized as the demand for a new, humanist ethics, with its taxing work and uncertain authority, Twain displays a longing for a way out. In *The Mysterious Stranger*, determinism functions as a plausible refuge from the plague of conscience, the "yaller dog" Huck Finn would rather poison than listen to. We are doomed to the knowledge of good and evil, and to the desperate ruses necessary to its evasion.

Such is the influence of the artist's Calvinist background, of the biblical tale of original sin, a narrative fundamental to Western philosophy, politics, and literature, which both Marx and Twain reference several times in their works. Humans are born into a fallen, guilty state, an endless loop of sin and repentance, in which the yearning for redemption struggles in vain against the tireless promptings of sin. This paradigm is central to understanding Twain's views of human nature, and by extension, human institutions, most especially economic relations involving labor, money, greed, and inequality. Though Twain vociferously rejects Christianity theology, its ethical models and logic underlie his critique of both American and international economic excesses. Traditional exegesis of Genesis explains our enduring sinfulness as a result of our fall from grace; every subsequent sin is a recapitulation of the original, another fall from the grace we can potentially repair with repentance and fortitude. The story portrays original sin as integral to our nature, which is greedy, receptive to opportunistic persuasions, and easy prey for the wiles of the serpent. Aptly, the biblical original sin is theft, and for both authors, theft, in simple or complex form, remains the most prominent of the social ills critiqued.

Our fall, even in myth, is an economic one. As punishment for stealing what was held back when so much was freely given, man would be forced to labor for the most basic needs. Capitalism is especially problematic under this logic. Earned money, utterly unnecessary in Eden, by its very existence reminds us of our original transgression; but the unearned surplus integral to capitalist success marks defiance of the divine penalty and a recapitulation of the archetypal sin of theft. Paul Taylor points out how deep this theme runs in American thought: "For the Puritans only earned material success could be taken as a sign of divine favor for the man who worked hard at his 'calling.' Thus unearned wealth is also stolen wealth, necessarily taken from someone who earned it. For their heirs in the nineteenth century unearned wealth was still suspected of being stolen."[15]

Both Marx and Twain mobilized origin stories to explain contemporary economic conditions, positing a prior state of grace in which humans were free of economic exploitation. Each imagines a fall from grace: Marx defines this directly as a descent from our true human nature, our "species-being," to a condition of alienation from our labor. For Marx, alienation is the ever-reproduced original sin, separating people from their real relation to their productivity. When our essential productivity in labor becomes labor-power, a commodity to be sold, it also becomes available for theft (as in the appropriation of surplus value and in other, more egregious forms), and theft is the immediate and inevitable consequence. Alienation from our labor thus corrupts human social relations, alienating us also from our true relations to each other and fostering the proliferation of economic and social hierarchies. Since alienation distorts the proper, natural relations between and among people and their labor, it invites and provokes the fetishization of economic elements, with the result that commodities, relationships, and people's economic identities are perverted.

The same principles operate in Twain, who figures the pre-alienation state as primitive yet edenic, as in child's play and in subsistence societies, where natural productivity is free of coercion. Economic exploitation, usually figured in theft, is a metonymic reproduction of original sin. While for individuals this is characterized as greed, frequently accompanied by evasive rationalizations obscuring its manifest immorality, in Twain's specific critiques of America the national original sin is the paired theft of Indian lands and slave labor. These form the dark background to a deformed and corrupting U.S. economy. These national crimes against humanity bear constant witness to the deficiencies of Americans' conventional morality, which provides no uncontaminated guidance for either Twain's characters or his contemporaries. These original thefts are regularly recalled and reiterated in troubled economic transactions in his fiction.

Twain's notorious aversion to work, which shows up in myriad ways both in his life and in his writing, exemplifies classic alienation from labor. Tom Sawyer's fence whitewashing provides a conspicuous illustration of the subject: Assigned the project as punishment, it is an alienated labor, done for and at the insistence of another, Aunt Polly. His friends, however, seduced by his pretended joy in the task, bring their full productive being to it, enjoying the labor as a satisfying end in itself, and even paying him for the privilege of pitching in. Tom, the ideal, benign capitalist, is deprived of the pleasures of his own productivity, reaping instead such excessive profit that "if he hadn't run out of whitewash he would have bankrupted every boy in the village" (*TS* 32). But his profits lead to the grave humiliation of being exposed as a cheat. Tom trades some of his ill-gotten wealth for tickets earned by other children as the reward for memorizing passages from the Bible. When Tom tries to cash in at church, his ignorance of the good book becomes the ironic occasion for a corrective lesson, established in Genesis, on the duty to labor for one's gain.

Twain's aphorism about the fence episode, "that work consists of whatever a body is obliged to do, and that play consists of whatever a body is not obliged to do" (*TS* 32), speaks to the coercive social relation—which the word *obliged* flags—central to alienation from one's "species-being" that Marx traces to the buying and selling of labor power. The playful exploration of the problem in *Tom Sawyer* contrasts with the bitter irony and anger in *Roughing It*, where Twain heaps scorn on Christian missionaries bringing the rewards of industrial labor to the indigenous Hawaiians. The missionaries "showed [them] what rapture it is to work all day long for fifty cents to buy food for the next day with, as compared to fishing for pastime and lolling in the shade through eternal Summer, and eating of the bounty that nobody labored to provide but Nature" (*RI* 463). Twain was evidently attracted to a subsistence economy, where a person's needs are satisfied through activity that is neither coerced nor inherently disagreeable: fishing for pastime. For Twain and Marx, our *natural* state is this unalienated Eden, an eternal Summer we should rightly wish to return to. For both, too, religious justification, Christianity in particular, is inextricably implicated in the fall from economic innocence. The missionaries introduce not only alienated work to the natives, but also the idea of eternal damnation, the ultimate alienation. Twain sarcastically laments "how sad it is to think of the multitudes who have gone to their graves in this beautiful island and never knew there was a hell" (*RI* 463).

Peoples, not just persons, are subject to alienation, as the process transforms societies as well as individuals. Twain recognized the possibility of an unalienated, purely use-value-centered economy primarily for those outside of civilization, which is defined in large part by its embrace of exchange value, private property, and the ritual of accumulation. As Twain notes in *Following the Equator*, native peoples living beyond the reach of Western civilization, whether in Hawaii, the American states, Australia, or India, are naturally subject to the impulse of greed, but enjoy shelter from the excesses of the market economy so long as they remain outside the orbit of its alienating mechanisms. As missionaries, settlers, and imperialists import the notion of private property, they simultaneously alter economies and human identity. Marx identifies the pre-contact state: "Cooperation, such as we find it at the dawn of human development, among races who live by the chase, or, say, in the agriculture of Indian communities, is based on the one hand, on ownership in common of the means of production, and on the other hand the fact that, in those cases, each individual has no more torn himself off from the navel-string of his tribe or community, than each bee has freed itself from the connection with the hive" (*MER* 387). Twain depicts the New World aftermath of this lost connection. The continued expropriation of Indian lands for private property in Twain's America creates the conspicuous alienation suffered by the unsettling figure of Injun Joe. The scorned half-breed is both without access to the means of production and "torn off" from any community. It is fitting, then, that his general craving for revenge has its principal focus in the judge who jailed him for the very state the community and country had imposed on him: vagrancy.

As the land theft figured in Injun Joe can represent half of America's nationally specific forces of alienation, of original sin, so the labor theft embodied in a slave can represent the other. While wage labor transforms human species-being—productive capacity—into exchange value, slavery transforms humans themselves, alienating people from their very species, their humanity. Twain illustrates this ultimate alienation when calling attention to slaves' monetary value. In *Life on the Mississippi* he observes of his childhood home that "at present rates, the people who occupy it are of no more value than I am; but in my time they would have been worth not less than five hundred dollars apiece. They are colored folk" (*LM* 537). Here the values of slavery merge ironically with broader evaluations of worth; the "colored folk" had only been worth *more* because they were morally valued at *less*. The former slaves' current worthlessness, in market terms, marks their pricelessness as people, at last beyond the reach of market valuation.

Both Marx and Twain observe that even true slavery has relatively more and less devastating levels of alienation: in more paternalistic versions, slaves are treated more as use values than as exchange values; when market forces prevail, their fate becomes horrific. Marx explains: "But as soon as people, whose production still moves within the lower forms of slave-labour, corvée labor, &c., are drawn into the whirlpool of an international market dominated by the capitalist mode of production, the sale of their products for export becoming their principal interest, the civilized horrors of over-work are grafted onto the barbaric horrors of slavery, serfdom &c. Hence the negro labor in the Southern States of the American Union preserved something of a patriarchal character, so long as production was chiefly directed to immediate local consumption." When the market offered profits through export, however, "the over-working of the negro and sometimes the using up of his life in seven years of labour became a factor in a calculated and calculating system" (*MER* 364–65). Twain directs us to this dynamic by looking at the moment when slaves' use value is being converted directly into exchange: when they are in the process of being sold, their commodification fully realized.

Such calculations are personalized in several places in *Huckleberry Finn*. Jim notes that Miss Watson "pecks on [him] all de time, en treats [him] pooty rough," but he does not run away since he is married, has children, and has ties to the community. Jim's humanity is stripped entirely away, moving him to run, only when Miss Watson is pushed to calculate his value, having been offered "sich a big stack o'money she couldn resis'" (*HF* 53) by a trader intent on exploiting Jim's exchange value. Scenes of slave trading are burned into Twain's and his characters' memories. In the emotional aftermath of the slave sale at Peter Wilks's house, Huck thinks both the white family and the slaves "would break their hearts for grief," saying, "I can't ever get it out of my memory" (*HF* 234). Huck here echoes Twain's own recollection of slaves he saw chained together "awaiting shipment to the Southern slave market" as "the saddest faces I have ever seen" (*AMT* 30). These scenes serve as painful reminders of what the ideology of paternalism can never fully obscure, the fundamentally economic nature of slavery, the alienation of individual and social human identity that it produces.

Along with observing his society's communal reiteration of alienation, Twain acquired intimate knowledge of it directly from personal experience, first as a laborer and later as a capitalist. In the Nevada silver fields he finds that he and other miners largely go hungry, ownership is ubiquitously dubious and subject to theft, and wealth is always accumulated through the exploitation of someone else. This is a particularly shocking revelation for the tenderfoot, as mining seems to promise a kind of free money apparently there for the taking, untouched by the corrupting human processes of exchange. In *Roughing It* Twain represents himself as initially so naive—like the reader whose eyes he will open— that he thinks of precious metals as essentially, naturally valuable, with no reliance on labor to realize their worth, quite the reverse of Marx's theory that while nature may provide the substratum for value, "labour is a creator of use-value . . . an eternal, nature-imposed necessity, without which there can be no material exchanges between man and Nature, and therefore no life" (*MER* 309). When his older brother Orion first tells him he is headed west, Twain enviously imagines that he "would see the gold mines and the silver mines, and maybe go about of an afternoon when his work was done, and pick up two or three pailfuls of shining slugs, and nuggets of gold and silver on the hillside" (*RI* 19). It comes as little surprise when Twain decides to join him.

What Twain finds, of course, and duly reports in *Roughing It*, is that the collective labor power necessary to extract value from the mines is distributed broadly, but that profits accrue to the very few (increasingly corporate bodies) who end up owning the mines. Laboring in mines is the losing part of the economic game, and he aspires to win, even while confessing that to do so is ethically troublesome. He becomes a speculator only after observing that others are "selling stock in their companies before they ever started drilling or making a profit," calling them "untechnical, leather-headed thieves" who planned "to be organized—at some indefinite period in the future—probably in time for the resurrection."[16] Eventually he has a capitalist revelation: "We had learned the *real* secret of success in silver mining—Which was, *not* to mine the silver ourselves by the sweat of our brows and the labor of our hands, but to *sell* the ledges to the dull slaves of toil and let them do the mining!" (*RI* 217). Twain sees an economic relation where he can be either victim or thief, and opts for the latter. His overt reference to the biblical injunction to labor—the wages of original sin being labor by the sweat of our brows and hands—marks his decision to become a speculator and salesman as a species of theft and an evasion of social responsibility.

Nineteenth-century Americans readily made this link. In his *Fables of Abundance*, T. J. Jackson Lears quotes Catherine Sedgwick's 1842 novel *Wilton Harvey*: "The curse of heaven has fallen upon those who make haste to be rich, forsaking toilsome enterprise, patient labour, and the appointed ways of ingenuity and industry for the legerdemain of visionaries and speculators."[17] The curse that commands us to labor also curses us if we do not obey. Twain's experiences as speculator, from the mines to the Paige typesetter, appear to corroborate this view.

Here, again, religion provides Twain's most accessible framework for discussing individual morality and social ethics. He was profoundly influenced by the capitalist system within which he operated. In attempting to evade the biblical injunction to labor by hiring others to mine silver for him, he reports embracing the role of exploiter that he has just critiqued, and his conspicuous use of the term *slaves of toil* imaginatively recruits him into an even more egregious system as he gives employment to, and profits from, slaves. Describing the miners as slaves fosters an implicit comparison of the economic systems of the antebellum South with the hyper-capitalist West, where in both cases ownership of the means of production, including the human instruments of slaves' bodies, is the "real secret" to success.

The "blind lead" episode in *Roughing It* highlights the relation between labor and rightful ownership. Twain and his companions finally locate a rich, valuable vein of ore outside of a large company's holdings, a section of rock that might yield significant profit. They are required by law to do a nominal amount of work on the lead to validate their claim. Through a series of suspicious coincidences suggesting some deliberate maneuvering to defraud them, they fail to labor as prescribed, and all except the one who defends his right with a cocked revolver lose their stake. The symbolic labor required implicitly acknowledges its imperative as a sign of fair ownership; the quantity expended is irrelevant. This symbolic ritual serves as an object lesson in the pairing of labor with rightful ownership, a relation Twain reviles yet reluctantly defends as he describes the clearly unjust uncoupling of the two in the chaotic economy of the silver bonanza.

As an alternative to either labor or ownership, Twain eventually recognizes a third way to live off the proceeds of this particular economy, and the American economy more largely: writing about it. As a journalist, he can sidestep direct involvement and still earn cash, a feat he celebrates most memorably when he brags that in writing about his father's bad investment in the Tennessee Lands, an ill-fated legacy (as it encouraged the Clemenses' reliance on prospective yet never-realized wealth), he was the only family member to realize a profit on it. Writing, however, could not be expected to provide the wealth and the leisure he desired, and so he continued an avowed and dedicated capitalist in his business life, even as he illustrated its destructive powers in his works.

Twain's lifelong attraction to capitalist speculation, even after it led to bankruptcy, verged on mania. As his secretary, Albert Bigelow Paine, wrote in a letter in the last year of the great humorist's life, "Business propositions of every sort—schemes, plans, investments, and the like . . . have been his undoing through a long period of years. He has never made an investment that brought him a return, however promising it seemed in the beginning. . . . But, as I have said, he is impulsive, enthusiastic, and likely to fall in with the suggestion of a plan which would only mean discomfort, worry, and nightmare for him later on."[18]

Paine was merely the first biographer to take note of Twain's obsession with the promise and the reality of wealth. What is most extraordinary is not that he shared the feverish zeal for capitalist speculation that, after all, fueled the postbellum period in American history during which he flourished, but that he did so while overtly acknowledging its irrationality, its deleterious effects on both the prospective capitalist and his labor force, and its harm to the culture as a whole. Justin Kaplan's acute observation that he "did write a kind of pornography of the dollar" directs us to the fetishization central to this obsession, one that Twain bestowed on so many of his characters, made central to the plots of his stories, and alluded to in the title of his novel *The Gilded Age*, which was readily adopted as a label for the period. Kaplan points out: "It is hard to think of another writer so obsessed in his life and work by the lure, the rustle and chink and heft of money. Silver is the Holy Grail of *Roughing It*. All but a few of the characters in *The Gilded Age* worship the golden calf; to possess money is to be religiously possessed; and money is the main character of that book in the same way that God is the main character of the Old Testament. Money corrupts Hadleyburg; the Mysterious Stranger poisons Eseldorf with it."[19]

Kaplan is surely correct that money in Twain's life and works replaces and subsumes the intensity of religious and sexual drives. Kaplan's observations neatly illustrate key features of fetishization, wherein the fetishized object or relation may be powerfully

exaggerated and intensified, transformed into new configura-
tions, displaced into other objects/relations; it may assume roles
far beyond its literal capabilities, occupying and using the powers
of entirely different things and forces. Commodity and money
fetishism fascinated both Twain and Marx. While Twain embodied them in his life and writing, Marx analyzed them as the
logical consequence of the money economy that emerges after
alienation converts labor into a commodity.

While comparing the crucial propositions the two make about
fetishization, it is useful to consider the stylistic differences that
inflect and shape their critiques. The stark difference between
Marx's systematic, scientific method and Twain's more scattered
and impressionistic approach may draw attention away from important similarities. Both deploy surface/depth and microcosm/
macrocosm models in treating socioeconomic problems; but
while Marx proceeds in a rationally ordered way, taking one logical and clearly defined step at a time, Twain is a literary stylist
whose stories, when closely examined, reveal insights and emergent positions bearing on American and international economics that closely parallel those of his European counterpart. The
American embodied ideas in characters, settings, and plotlines—
sometimes quite consciously and overtly, at other times hap-
hazardly—through symbol, metaphor, and developed thematic
patterns. Both writers explored economics by examining external features and by mining into the deeper foundations, the underlying structures, assumptions, and forces that left few traces
on surface phenomena. Fetishization, one such hidden element,
by its very nature lends itself to literary representation. Inherently a creative process, it invests its objects with greater meanings
and frequently involves representational modes including sym-
bolism, metaphor, and paradox. Literature and fetishism share
a propensity to imaginatively transform and enhance the mun-
dane, and conversely, to reveal in the ordinary its hidden dimensions: the latent, the occult, the extraordinary.

As a philosopher and political economist, Marx systematically hypothesized, made propositions, then backed them with
reasoning, evidence, and illustration. Depending on your orien-

tation, his approach may appear to be admirably or maddeningly abstract. He defines commodity fetishism thus: "The mysterious character of the commodity-form consists therefore simply in the fact that the commodity reflects the social characteristics of men's own labour as objective characteristics of the products of labour themselves, as the socio-natural properties of these things. . . . It is nothing but the definite social relation between men themselves that assumes here, for them, the fantastic form of a relation between things. . . . I call this the fetishism which attaches itself to the products of labor as soon as they are produced as commodities, and is therefore inseparable from the production of commodities" (C 165). In short, the commodity's value seems to arise not from the human production of it, but from its current form as object. Fetishization occurs when the true social nature of human labor is turned into objects exchanged for money, which then makes them appear to be in trade with each other, disguising the underlying social relations mediating the exchange. How humans have created that value is rendered invisible. This is the same conundrum Twain puzzles out in the silver fields, initially assuming that ore possesses an inherent, natural value, only to find an economy based not in metal, but in the churning social dynamics of labor, force, and ownership. His approach renders the analysis both palatable and potent, but also readily overlooked, a characteristic that almost certainly made his work more popular than Marx's.

Notwithstanding his commitment to order and logic, Marx also recognizes the value of literature as an illustrative enhancement of scientific argument. In his "Economic and Philosophic Manuscripts of 1844" he quotes and explicates Goethe and Shakespeare as illustrative of the magical, fetishized nature of money itself, a matter vital in many of Twain's novels. Marx's commentary explores how money not only attains supernatural status, but also how it infiltrates and supersedes human identity itself. A passage in Goethe's *Faust* inspires him to generalize: "By possessing the property of buying everything . . . money is thus the object of eminent possession. The universality of its property is the omnipotence of its being. It therefore functions as the almighty being. Money is the pimp between man's need and the object, between his life and his means of life. But that which mediates my life for me, also mediates the existence of other people for me. For me it is the other person" (*MER* 103).

He finds, after considering Shakespeare, who "excellently depicts the real nature of money," that money substitutes not only for the other, but also for the self: "That for which I can pay, that I am. . . . Money's properties are my properties and essential powers—the properties and powers of its possessor." Thus, he continues, if people can alter the effects of their personal characteristics—ugliness, lameness, stupidity, even dishonesty—through money, then they are, in effect, no longer those things. "The overturning and confounding of all human and natural qualities, the fraternization of impossibilities—the divine power of money—lies in its character as men's estranged, alienating and self-disposing species-nature. Money is the alienated ability of mankind" (*MER* 104).

What Marx has proposed here, Twain intuits; and arguments that Marx develops systematically, Twain imparts intermittently, by fits and starts, and at varying levels of intentionality, across the mingled surface of his prose. Money is magical and nearly omnipotent. No wonder he covets vast fortunes; no wonder Tom Sawyer hunts treasure. Money perverts relationships and usurps our identities. No wonder Twain keeps pairing it with murder and death; no wonder Huck tries to give away the "awful sight of money" he digs out of Injun Joe's grave. The author cannot help catching sight of the warning, the threatened loss of social connection and human identity in money's "confounding" operations. How could anyone who had lived through slavery—which literalized the confounding of men and money in the slave trade—avoid such ominous intimations?

Jim gives expression to these wonderful and fearsome qualities outright when he paradoxically empowers himself with the omnipotence of his dollar value. After "stealing" himself from slavery, he claims what Marx would have called his "alienated abilities" by invoking his monetary worth: "I's rich now, come to look at it. I owns mysef, en I's wuth eight hund'd dollars" (*HF* 57). Huck is less sanguine about the price on his head; for as long as he possesses the six thousand dollars in treasure, his father will continue to pursue him. When Pap, by virtue of paternity and kidnapping, possesses Huck, who is commensurate with the treasure, he feels entitled to the fortune and curses those who will not treat him according to this measure of his worth. "The law," he rants, "takes a man worth six-thousand dollars and upards, and jams him into an old log cabin like this, and lets him go round in clothes that ain't fitten for a hog" (*HF* 33). The commutative power of money, which makes man exchangeable with other goods, and even with other men, here condemns Huck to a state closely resembling Jim's, captive because of his cash value and liable to the whims of both a master and American law. The economics of slavery reveals an even more widespread pattern of fetishization in the America of Twain's creation.

Marx outlines how capitalism's promise of self-reproducing money—which "brings forth living offspring, or at least lays golden eggs" (*C* 255), and whereby investment rather than labor seems to be the engine of productivity—fosters this fetish. It is a promise erected, of course, on alienated labor, without which any surplus value a worker creates would accrue to its creator, the worker. We have already observed such fetishization in *Roughing It*—both in its fantasies of laborless success and in its imagery of piles of silver and gold—and in its author's fervid acquisitiveness. Twain imagines his father's vision of the Tennessee lands as positively alchemical: "I will not live to see these acres turn to silver and gold, but my children will" (*AMT* 22). The human role—labor, hands, and sweat—has no place in his fantastic scheme. But one need look no further than Colonel Sellers, as he appears in *The Gilded Age* and *The American Claimant*, for the consummate embodiment of the fetishist.

The underlying pattern of fetishization, where human agency is suppressed from economic acts and states, emerges regardless of stylistic differences between the thinkers' approaches. Like Marx's more direct investigations, Twain's literalization of money fetishism provides a view into its complex and sordid backstory. When Tom Sawyer leaves a nickel on a counter to "pay" for candles he stole while playing a trick on Jim, the coin is a repository of meanings. It is both capital and a charm by which Jim can make money and, purportedly, tell the future, and an amulet, reminding Jim of his value and capacity for productive work for himself, leading him to become "most ruined for a servant" (*HF* 8) and thereby prompting him to run away, catalyzing the plot. Tom employs it as a fetish item, calling on it to transform theft into fair exchange; instead the nickel marks—while it is simultaneously marshaled to excuse—Tom's theft and cruelty. (His maliciousness is revealed in his plans to tie Jim to a tree, foiled when Huck persuades him to mitigate the "joke" by hanging Jim's hat on the tree instead.) If we look to the coin's past we find it most likely derived from the fortune Tom stole from Injun Joe, a fortune he will split with Huck, much of which was stolen from Murrel's gang of homicidal slave traders, who "earned" it in the course of selling and killing runaway slaves. The story reveals a submerged but acute critique of American economics, from its origins in racial strife and dispossession to its promises of freedom and self-possession.

The two elements of fetishized currency that Twain employs to set off Huck and Jim's journey are complexly interwoven: the coin Jim now wears is probably culled from the larger fortune of gold (formerly Injun Joe's) that curses Huck. The treasure at the heart of the Tom Sawyer and Huck Finn novels leads us back from proximate causes to more ultimate questions: How did it come to be that Tom started free and with cash, while Jim was enslaved and penniless? How do classes and castes develop? Why are societies so frequently characterized by vast economic disparities? The money synecdochically represents not only the economy in which it currently functions, but also the economy it was derived from, whose wealth is the guilty return on stealing from and killing Indians (Injun Joe's death significantly facilitates the transfer of capital) and a homicidal trade in slaves, piously sanctioned by church and state. The relatively simple obscuring of human agency that fetishization provides gives way to the colossal ideology buttressing inequality in America (and as Twain makes clear in other works, worldwide), where earlier, foundational displacements and dispossessions—massacres, murders, appropriations, and robberies—are rebranded as both destiny and blessing. This parallels and illustrates Marx's revised theory of "primitive accumulation."

Marx asserts that conventional political economy explains wealth disparities in relatively developed societies in a myth about sin and goodness, which aligns with and supersedes theology's original sin:

> Long, long ago there were two sorts of people; one, the diligent, intelligent, and above all frugal elite; the other, lazy rascals, spending their substance, and more, on riotous living. . . . Thus it came to pass that the former sort accumulated wealth, and the latter sort finally had nothing to sell but their own skins. And from this original sin dates the poverty of the great majority who, despite all their labour, have up to now nothing to sell but themselves, and the wealth of the few that increases constantly, although they have long since ceased to work. (*C* 873)

Just as each of their descendants has to carry the weight of Adam and Eve's disobedience in spite of not having partaken of the apple, so descendants of the lazy and profligate suffer the sins of their fathers. Unspoken here, but understood, is that we share the characteristics of our forebears. Thus people get what they deserve, both by the terms of historical justice and as the inevitable consequence of their differing natures. Colonial expansion, imperialism, and slavery take recourse in this mythology, which not only valorizes might and wealth, but also attests to the salutary effects of forced labor on those not destined, by their nature or history, to ownership and the pleasures of accumulation. Marx's rebuttal of this story, which "is everyday preached to us in the defence of property," challenges this pernicious doctrine with analysis drawn from the real, rather than mythic, past. "In actual history, it is a notorious fact that conquest, enslavement, robbery, murder, in short, force, play the greatest part" (*C* 874) in the early processes of accumulation underpinning modern economies. The real "pre-history of capital," he asserts, "is nothing more than the historical process of divorcing the producer from the means

of production" (*C* 875). Thus primitive accumulation culmi-
nates in private property, by which Marx means ownership of the
means of production. Private property is a fetish item, concealing
as it does the "dead labor" accumulated in it—the surplus value
or profit that is not distributed to the producers but is instead
held as capital—which thereby also signals theft.

Twain's works reflect and critique his culture's reliance on this
myth's characterizations of the "two sorts of people," along with
the accompanying psycho/sociological rationalization, the ideology of merit, demonstrating how it sits at the center of concentric levels of self-justification, from individuals and communities
to nations and international alliances. *The Prince and the Pauper*
and *Pudd'nhead Wilson* overtly deconstruct the myth, their plots
relying on their respective societies' inability to actually tell the
two types apart. It seems that the "sorts" are as interchangeable
as clothes, the bodies that wear these distinctive markers virtually twins. In these stories, the conventional legend of primitive
accumulation reveals itself as a fetish, a reification of human-
created divisions. The human types that Marx's myth characterizes as the diligent (who will become owners) and the lazy (who
will be reduced to wage laborers) correspond closely to other bi-
furcations of the worthy and unworthy: aristocrats and peasants,
the civilized and the savage, masters and slaves. These categories
are readily superimposed on one another, and those on one side
can recall the others while substituting for them. Alan Trachtenberg notes this conflation in the dean of Yale Law School's description of the newly poor "tramps" of the 1870s: "As we utter
the word Tramp, there arises straightaway before us the spectacle
of a lazy, incorrigible, cowardly, utterly depraved savage."[20] Civilized or savage, rich or poor, their positions in the social hierarchy are deemed the result of shared character traits that Marx
and Twain, in their different ways, interpret as post hoc rationalizations mobilized to justify social inequality. Twain's shuffling
of the opposed types exposes a distinction without a difference.
Huck, though white, through his abject poverty is aligned with
slaves and the peasantry and the savage, which also puts him in
company with Injun Joe, whose literal legacy, the six thousand

dollars in gold, haunts and endangers him. Aristocrats and masters converge in those extravagant frauds, the king and the duke, who blithely take possession of both Huck and Jim. Their parody of aristocratic privilege and style makes a mockery of the hierarchy they aspire to. In the course of his attempt to ease Jim's fears about the excesses of European royalty, Huck observes of the odious tricksters on board the raft that "you couldn't tell them from the real kind" (*HF* 201), and thus collapses the highly reified class distinction between rich and poor.

As Twain, like Marx, exposes the foundations of class as arbitrary and unnatural, he looks to the decadent European model of social privilege so visible in *The Prince and the Pauper* and *A Connecticut Yankee*, but also often foregrounds, in works like *Pudd'nhead Wilson* and "To the Person Sitting in Darkness," the American and imperialist contexts that mix and overlay class with racialized designations of worth. Twain has Hank Morgan, in *A Connecticut Yankee*, elucidate the common core quite neatly:

> The blunting effects of slavery upon the slaveholder's moral perceptions are known and conceded, the world over, and a privileged class, an aristocracy, is but a band of slaveholders by another name. . . . One needs but hear an aristocrat speak of the classes that are below him to recognize—and in but indifferently modified measure—the very air and tone of the actual slaveholder; and behind these are the slaveholder's spirit, the slaveholder's blunted feeling. These are the result of the same cause, in both cases: the possessor's old and inbred custom of regarding himself as a superior being. (*CY* 316)

Privileged classes mistakenly view their privilege as the result of inherent worth; property must reflect diligence, and poverty, laziness. Marx asserts that the capitalist mode of production mechanistically supports this notion of superiority as "the relations of production themselves create a new relation of supremacy and subordination (and this also has a political expression)" (*C* 1027). The roles played out under capitalism are adduced as evidence supporting the myth of capital's origins. But Twain and

Marx argue that this gets things backward: a belief in one's worthiness is a common result of privilege, and not, as ideological rationalizing would have it, the other way around. Twain makes this point in *The Mysterious Stranger,* where it is clearly suggested that plausible reasons can be constructed to justify almost anything; and again in "The Man That Corrupted Hadleyburg," where self-righteous townspeople concoct false memories and pretexts in order to persuade themselves that they are entitled to a sack of gold.

Slavery is the lowest point on the continuum of social hierarchy primed by the myth of primitive accumulation. In *A Connecticut Yankee*, Hank notes that subscribing to an ideology subjects one to it: "The most of King Arthur's British nation were slaves, pure and simple, and bore that name and wore the iron collar on their necks, and the rest were slaves in fact, but without the name." Force has created the pure slaves, but the ideology of class hierarchy enslaves the others, the "rabbits" who faithfully believe in the inherent superiority of their social betters. Hank goes on to lay bare the central goals of the feudal economy:

> The truth was, the nation as a body was in the world for one object, and one only: to grovel before king and Church and noble; to slave for them, sweat blood for them, starve that they might be fed, work that they might play, drink misery to the dregs that they might be happy, go naked that they might wear silks and jewels, pay taxes that they might be spared from paying them, be familiar all their lives with the degrading language and postures of adulation that they might walk in pride and think themselves the gods of this world. (*CY* 98)

Twain elsewhere tries out alternative explanations for social hierarchy. In *Life on the Mississippi*, ruminating on the nonsensical admiration, and even nostalgia, among Southerners for hierarchical societies, he comes to the view that much of the blame must fall on Sir Walter Scott. A great reductionist move, this is one of Twain's most startling and also most optimistic moments, as it suggests a simple solution to a profound social conundrum—

the belief in inherently inferior and superior peoples—that has elsewhere stymied him. Scott, Twain insists, "created rank and caste down there, and also reverence for rank and caste, and pride and pleasure in them" (*LM* 469). As they are romantically represented in Scott's popular historical novels, rank and caste deform human interpersonal relations and set up false distinctions, which, Twain argues, were widely influential in the South during the several decades before the Civil War. By this logic, Scott is responsible not for slavery itself, but for the "Southern character," which, Twain clearly implies, warmed to slavery as the sine qua non of aristocratic social life. Scott reinforced Southerners' delusions of slaveholding's nobility and gentility in romanticized visions of feudal societies.

Twain seems to be proposing that had the influence of Scott's novels been better understood, the culture it reinforced might have atrophied and even disappeared, thus drawing into focus the underlying economic realities of slavery. As Marx believed that the revolutionary truth of his scientific analysis of economics would bring enlightenment to the masses, so Twain hoped that his treatment of Scott, and other pernicious influences, would open eyes and change minds. He had seen it happen before. "A curious exemplification of the power of a single book for good or harm," he argues, "is shown in the effects wrought by *Don Quixote* and those wrought by *Ivanhoe*. The first swept the world's admiration for the medieval chivalry-silliness out of existence; and the other restored it. As far as our South is concerned, the good work done by Cervantes is pretty nearly a dead letter, so effectually has Scott's pernicious work undermined it" (*LM* 470).

The confidence reflected in this analysis resurfaces in the revolutionary trajectory of *A Connecticut Yankee*, Twain's literary refutation of Scott and homage to Cervantes. Its hero Hank Morgan finds that there may indeed be two human types, but that they have been sorted into utterly irrelevant categories, aristocrat or peasant, whereas his Yankee egalitarianism directs him to the truly—rather than conventionally—worthy, whom he sets to uplifting in his "man-factories." Like his creator, Hank admires capitalism's ability to topple entrenched class distinctions.

Trachtenberg notes that for many during this period, "all producers seemed potential entrepreneurs, and workers 'nascent
capitalists.'"[21] Hank effects some capitalist reforms, brings in
advertising, and dreams of a progressive revolution not unlike
Marx's, with proletarian rule (but small-scale capitalism as the
economic engine): "First, a modified monarchy, till Arthur's days
were done, then the destruction of the throne, nobility abolished,
every member of it bound to some useful trade, universal suf-
frage instituted, and the whole government placed in the hands
of the men and women of the nation, there to remain" (*CY* 391).

But Twain becomes increasingly uneasy about the plot he has
set in motion, which has—as his plots so often do—verged away
from the course he seems clearly to have intended for it. As Fred
Kaplan points out, Hank "finds himself in a colonialist's paradise,"
where he has a monopoly on development.[22] He welcomes the
opportunity to become "the Boss," a position of greater real power than the king's. Hank fancies himself an enlightened despot,
but his self-aggrandizing nature contrasts with his avowed egalitarianism. Hank's gradual transformation into a colonialist—
he consolidates power, smites enemies thoughtlessly, and se-
cures his authority through quick-witted deceits and technological magic—triggers Twain's increasing discomfort. After Hank
sets up that ultimate capitalist tool, the stock market, his creator, in a telling historical revision, assigns the decline of the
kingdom as much to Launcelot's exploits in the market as to his
imprudent affair with the queen. When the Church takes over,
Hank still believes that his revolution will succeed, but soon
finds, to his dismay, that education is no match for upbringing in the formation of political ideology. When his second-
in-command asks, "Did you think you had educated the super-
stition out of those people?" Hank replies, "I certainly did think
it," only to be told, "Well, then, you may unthink it" (*CY* 538).
With scant regard for the novelist's conscious intentions, *A Connecticut Yankee* illustrates that it is more difficult to uproot Scott,
rank, and caste than Twain and his hero had anticipated.

Hank, as capitalist, imperialist, and insurgent, fails to account
for the fact that the same problems of human nature, supersti-

tion, and ideology that rule the sixth still hold sway in the nineteenth century. The Church may be the power responsible for his new society's downfall, but the people are its instrument. Though the players in the two historical settings are different, Hank faces a danger inherent to colonialists and revolutionaries: educational indoctrination to a new regime may be potent, yet it is nonetheless insufficient to sustain a revolution, in part at least because the technologies of the new regime, including its massive machinery of death, could be used against it. Facing the probability that his weapons will fall into the hands of his enemies, Hank stages a mini-apocalypse, obliterating the institutions and repositories of the revolutionary civilization he has created. He manages to kill twenty-five thousand members of the aristocracy, but then finds himself surrounded by concentric rings of rotting corpses and bereft of a popular following. Hemmed in by a "trap of [his] own making" (CY 570), he is forced to concede that his revolution has failed to change the fundamental course of history.

Twain thus exposes the arbitrariness of rank and caste and the absurdity of reverence for it, but illustrates at the same time its ubiquity and the durability of its social foundation. He recalls the evils of feudalism and slavery, but finds that enlightened nineteenth-century ideas and military technology are inadequate to their eradication. His disenchantment both with politics and with human nature would deepen further with the rise of American imperialism at century's end. Such is the clear message of *Following the Equator*, the record of his trip in 1896 around the world. He finds that dogmas of superiority are global phenomena, fueling both pre-capitalist and contemporary, first-world practices. The brutal realities of capitalism and its prehistory in America that appear in veiled form in his novels and stories—for example, in the genocide hinted at by Injun Joe's deeds and death—are much more openly exposed in the long travel book. In the West's territorial possessions, the myth and reality of primitive accumulation operate in full force and in full view.

While Marx regarded primitive economic forms as stages in an historical continuum, Twain viewed them as manifestations of a permanent state. Richard Miller points out that Marx treats the

myriad forms of primitive accumulation as parallel forms in the
ongoing process of capitalism's growth and decline:

> In Marx's view the initial proliferation of large-scale capitalist
> manufacturing enterprises depended on enormous and concen-
> trated profits from the imperial expansion that culminated in the
> first British empire. The discovery of gold and silver in America,
> the extirpation, enslavement and entombment in mines of the in-
> digenous population of that continent, the beginnings of the con-
> quest and plunder of India, and the conversion of Africa into a
> preserve for the commercial hunting of black skins, are all things
> which characterize the dawn of the era of capitalist production.[23]

In *Following the Equator,* Twain's narrative closely parallels
Marx's assessment of the real process of accumulating wealth,
taking note of contemporary as well as historical genocides, massacres, enslavement, and land-grabbing, frequently accompanied
by conversions to those Siamese twins, Christianity and Civilization. He notes that the people of the Pacific Islands seem to have
the unenviable choice between being press-ganged into slavery
and likely death, or consigned to population collapse, remarking
that for the Hawaiian native, "exile to Queensland—with the opportunity to acquire civilization, an umbrella, and a pretty poor
quality of profanity—is twelve times as deadly for him as war.
Common Christian charity, common humanity, does seem to
require that these people be returned to their homes, but that
war, pestilence, and famine be introduced among them for their
preservation" (*FE* 88–89). He surveys the tragic depopulation of
the Melbourne tribes with similarly bitter irony: "The white man
knew ways of reducing a population 80 percent in 20 years. The
native had never seen anything so fine" (*FE* 208–9).

The ideology rationalizing and sanctifying such barbarous
dispossession disturbed him almost as deeply as the acts themselves. He ironically praises the direct poisoning, in one case, and
burning to death, in another, of different groups of natives as
merciful compared to the "customary" methods, "robbery, humiliation, and slow, slow murder through poverty and the white

man's whiskey." Poisoning a tribe's pudding "tried to introduce the element of mercy into the superior race's dealings with the savage" (*FE* 213). Discussing South Africa, he outlines a philosophy that might be brought to bear more broadly on the civilized Western policy in relation to other lands: "The great bulk of the savages must go. The white man wants their lands, and all must go excepting such percentage of them as he will need to do his work for him upon terms to be determined by himself. Since history has removed the element of guesswork from this matter and made it certainty, the humanest way of diminishing the black population [direct genocide] should be adopted, not the old cruel ways of the past" (*FE* 690). These deeds, he notes repeatedly, spread the blessings of civilization and are sustained by the confident belief in the superiority of the people and culture of the Western world. Self-deception, as much as greed, is responsible for belief in a meritocracy founded in fiction, plain and simple; the same blunt logic applies when it comes to laying blame for the resulting human atrocities. Though he had proved himself entirely vulnerable to both self-deception and greed, Twain was bold to inveigh against them, noting (in his role as jester) that "there are many humorous things in the world; among them the white man's notion that he is less savage than other savages" (*FE* 213). Twain thus clearly agreed with Marx that only one sort of person exists. They disagreed just as clearly on what sort of person that is.

The problem with human history, Twain insists, is humans. We are perennial thieves engaged in perennial theft: "All the territorial possessions of all the political establishments in the earth—including America, of course—consist of pilferings from other people's wash. No tribe, howsoever insignificant, and no nation, howsoever mighty, occupies a foot of land that was not stolen" (*FE* 323). Land stolen once will inevitably be stolen again, as the world powers were then proving as they skirmished over colonial holdings. Twain makes feeble stabs at hopefulness, but can sustain Marx's species of optimism only in brief intervals. In *Life on the Mississippi*, he looks with approval on revolutionary progress: "Against the crimes of the French Revolution and of Bonaparte may be set two compensating benefactions: the Revolution broke the chains of the *ancien régime* and of the Church, and made a nation of abject slaves a nation of freemen" (*LM* 467). But this flicker of light soon gives way to an angry diatribe on the regressive influence of Sir Walter Scott. As History plays itself out, Twain declares, "the savage lands of the world are to pass to alien possession, their peoples at the mercy of alien rulers. Let us hope and believe that they will benefit by the change" (*FE* 626). But how little hope his ironic "let us hope" actually conveys!

While Twain was in agreement with Marx about the problems of human history, the strong skeptical trend in his thinking runs counter to Marx's progressivist view. Though Marx may have acknowledged some chronological overlap, he was nonetheless steadfast in proposing that primitive accumulation was an earlier form than capitalism, that the advent of capitalism's unique array of abuses was already underway and would continue to supersede earlier forms, and that, as the result, the revolution of the proletariat was inevitable. Twain not only doubted that a revolution was coming, but feared that he would lose his head if it did. Such important differences notwithstanding, our paired writers were insightful explorers who showed how closely human identity is tied to productivity and work, to social value as well as economic worth, and how easily it is deformed by unequal power relations. They powerfully illuminated our everyday transactions with things and other people, and the array of forces—economic, social, psychological, political—working on and through us. They continue to challenge us to scrutinize our beliefs and possessions, and above all our relations with one another. If Marx envisioned history as a march forward, for Twain it was a dance, not always linear or pretty to watch, but engaging and consuming. Where Marx exhorted us to throw off our chains, Twain warned us to watch our step.

NOTES

1. On the authority of unconscious motives in Twain's writing, see Forrest G. Robinson, "An 'Unconscious and Profitable Cerebration':

Mark Twain and Literary Intentionality," *Nineteenth-Century Literature* 50 (1995): 357–80.

2. Biographical materials on Marx are drawn from David McLellan, *Karl Marx: His Life and Thought,* and Vincent Barnett, *Marx;* on Twain from Justin Kaplan, *Mr. Clemens and Mark Twain,* and Jerome Loving, *Mark Twain: The Adventures of Samuel L. Clemens.*

3. Loving, *Mark Twain: The Adventures of Samuel L. Clemens,* 304.

4. William Dean Howells, "My Mark Twain," 310.

5. For a full discussion of the debate on Marx the moralist, see Jeffrey Reiman, "Moral Philosophy: The Critique of Capitalism and the Problem of Ideology."

6. From Twain's notebook for 1895, as cited in Henry Nash Smith, *Mark Twain: The Development of a Writer* (Cambridge: Harvard University Press, 1962), 203.

7. For a broad representation of Twain's views on the subject, see *Mark Twain on the Damned Human Race,* ed. Janet Smith (New York: Hill and Wang, 1962).

8. Roger B. Salomon, *Twain and the Image of History,* 126.

9. For a much fuller treatment, see John McMurtry, *The Structure of Marx's World-View,* 19–53.

10. Ibid., 32–33.

11. Richard W. Miller, "Social and Political Theory: Class, State, Revolution." 73.

12. Terence Ball, "History: Critique and Irony," 139.

13. Albert Bigelow Paine, *Mark Twain: A Biography,* 4:1296.

14. T. J. Jackson Lears, *No Place of Grace,* 41.

15. Paul Taylor, "The Education of a Young Capitalist," 343.

16. Quoted in Peter Krass, *Ignorance, Confidence and Filthy Rich Friends,* 29.

17. T. J. Jackson Lears, *Fables of Abundance,* 58.

18. Hamlin Hill, *Mark Twain God's Fool,* 259.

19. Kaplan, *Mr. Clemens and Mark Twain,* 96.

20. Alan Trachtenberg, *The Incorporation of America,* 71.

21. Ibid., 75.

22. Fred Kaplan, afterword to *Following the Equator,* by Mark Twain, 10.

23. Miller, "Social and Political Theory," 95.

Conclusion

CATHERINE CARLSTROEM

Man is the only animal that blushes. Or needs to.

> —Mark Twain, Pudd'nhead Wilson's
> New Calendar, *Following the Equator*

Mark Twain's folk wisdom as an observer of human nature and societies has long been recognized; the ubiquity of quotations from his works and maxims testifies to the acuity and abiding relevance of his wit, particularly for Americans, but also throughout the world. Yet emphasis on his folksiness, on the clarity and accessibility of his ideas, has served to obscure their foundations in and contributions to fields including sociology, psychology, philosophy, politics, and economics, provinces ceded to systematic scholars like our sages. His scattershot, intuitive approach may camouflage his insights, but his serious critiques and inquiries in these areas consistently shape his works nonetheless, as vibrant, fundamental elements. For the most part, this has worked out well for Twain, preserving his popularity and selling, even today, a great many of his books, but at a cost. The jester, because he is so easily dismissed as fool, his observations shrugged off as amusing but trivial, can say with near impunity what others are censured or marginalized for, his incisiveness protected by society's deliberate underestimation of him. The pithy humor of his critiques renders them at once highly valued and diminished.

Our study, we hope, helps explain how Twain occupies this equivocal position in the popular imagination, as well as some of his extraordinary appeal. Exploring his affinities with Nietzsche, Freud, and Marx—from whom no direct lines of influence extend—allows us to reckon with and reassess the interplay of his works with the period's most profound and substantive concerns: social morality, the role of the conscience, the mysteries of consciousness, and the causes and consequences of vast material inequalities. Thus we can know Twain better. Conversely, we can also know ourselves better. By recognizing and exploring his works' convergences with these others' "European" ideas, we can see more clearly the ideas' pervasiveness in nineteenth-century America. Twain's position as an iconic figure, one whose preoccupations have been widely understood to reflect his countrymen's, underlines the significance of these theories and problems in an American context, while simultaneously reminding us of the international scope of even his seemingly parochial musings.

By investigating the same works through the lenses of different sages—for example, exploring in sections of *Huckleberry Finn* both Freud's thoughts on the uncanny and Marx's concept of alienation—we see parallels emerging between the Europeans' ideas as well. That he quips, theorizes, dramatizes, and ruminates on subjects central to the works of the others, we have already argued throughout this book; having reviewed his consonance with them individually, we now turn to reconsider his accord with our sages collectively. Twain's works drew connections, overtly in lectures and speeches and in more veiled forms in the theater of his fiction, between areas—cultural, psychological, and material forces—which the others treated primarily as individual phenomena. The epigram above serves as a brief illustration of his works' power to coalesce around and resonate with fertile concepts that preoccupy the others. The American's aphorism on man's propensity to blush, presumably because he "needs to" recognize his own wrongdoing or inadequacy, encompasses and gives way to the Europeans' broader schemas of self-consciousness, moral transgression, and guilt.

Twain's grappling with social obligations and bondage to conventional morality, as well as both personal and communal guilt, sets theories of *ressentiment*, conceptions of the punitive role of the superego, and myths of capitalist entitlement alongside each other. Nietzsche might explain the blush through notions of slave-morality and subjugation to a life-sapping *ressentiment*, denial of an affirming, noble ethics beyond conventions of good and evil. For Freud it might represent the superego's censure of the self-indulgent id, for Marx, the individual's recognition of complicity in inequality and the self-delusion of alienation.

The saying functions as a microcosm of Twain's guilt-obsessed corpus, where these thinkers' renderings of the blush—humans wrestling with conscience—are at play. We are reminded of Nietzsche when *No. 44, The Mysterious Stranger*'s Satan proposes an end to blushing, first in determinism, then, ultimately, in a nihilism that suggests all others are merely imaginary, figments to whom one can have no ethical obligations. Twain's Freudian solution—murdering his conscience outright (like one might an overbearing father)—leads to rule by the id and the satisfying if impractical solution of a massacre in "The Facts Concerning the Recent Carnival of Crime in Connecticut." Marxian criticism is evoked not only in the fetishization of money in *Huckleberry Finn* but also on the raft, where Twain can briefly imagine an idyllic place free of market valuations of human worth. In every case, the writers investigate a question fundamental to all societies: what do we owe one another? They analyze the demands of a social ethics and the limits of self-understanding in an age of uncertain moral authority and rapidly changing political and economic structures.

These changing social structures have their analog in the individual as society acquires a greater appreciation of the complexity of the human mind even while confronting a sense of that mind as newly divided and fragmented. Our authors are all witness to emergent conceptions of the unconscious, a mysterious force surging toward the discordant surfaces of modern life. They seek to understand the hidden, buried, or repressed aspects of human experience, conflicts within as well as between people, and to see also how these may be reflected in beliefs and institutions. They observe, catalog, and critique different but interlinked forms of false consciousness looming over our selves and our societies: *ressentiment*, repression, alienation, the moral sense, and the lie of silent assertion.

For the sages and the jester, society itself is an ineluctable source of inner—and outer—conflict. Like Nietzsche, Twain, in many places—from his slaying of his conscience to Huck's decision to go to hell—seems to reject notions of good and evil, as they are corrupted by culture and burden the conscience intolerably. Yet Twain's abstract nihilism is countered by a call for moral reform in the face of concrete, real human interaction, including the material conditions so central to Marx's analysis. Twain's works ultimately reject the notion that one type of person is above the ethical obligations of the masses, even while acknowledging the inadequacy of any codified morality. While Freud and Twain agree that consciousness is suffering, in Twain this flows from palpable knowledge of and guilt over others' pain. While others' pain takes as many forms as there are individuals, Twain's work notes that much of it is due to imbalances of economics and power. Thus Freud's and Twain's mutual love of the idea of oblivion is linked to the ubiquitous and seemingly eternal problem of class inequality that so occupied Marx.

Twain may wish his conscience dead, and fantasize about killing it, but it will not die, in spite of his ratiocinations. Even the most solipsistic line in *No 44, The Mysterious Stranger*, "Dream other dreams, and better" (*MS* 404), resonates with an idealistic impulse, the drive to reformulate the world along new lines. *Better*, after all, is the comparative case of *good*, an inescapably moral word choice. Twain not only reckons with guilt personally but is compelled to act—regardless of both his own and his nation's attempts at evasion—as a collective conscience for his society.

But what might inspire this set of authors to unanimously determine that society so clearly needs to blush, that it needs a new conscience, a new perspective on morality? As we have stated previously, the social, political, and intellectual tumult of the nineteenth century was accompanied by a widespread crisis of authority. The death of God, who had served as a simple answer to the question of the origins of human conditions, catalyses all of our thinkers' subsequent inquiry. Like Nietzsche, Freud, and Marx, Twain focuses in his musings on the primacy of humans as creators of their own cultures, institutions, beliefs, and selves— in short, on their role as makers of their own realities. All four thinkers scrutinize and reject religious frameworks that had previously explained man's proper roles, relations, mind and spirit, and material circumstances. For Nietzsche this involves direct repudiation of Judeo-Christian morality, seen as valorizing weakness and negativity, and a return to an imagined pre-Christian state of consciousness, a natural, affirming, instinctive realm of power, free of the passivity that accepting God's will engenders. Freud's exploration of forces at work in the human psyche, most especially the frequently contending id, ego, and superego, replaced the conventional understanding of inward contests between good and evil, sinfulness and virtue. Marx chastises and instructs a civilization that had come to accept vast inequality, exploitation, and economic crimes like race- and wage-slavery as manifestations of God's will and reflections of a divinely inspired, predestined hierarchy.

Twain's work is driven throughout his oeuvre by similar impulses to rethink religious cosmology, to interrogate conventional constructions of consciousness and conscience, and to challenge the unjust distribution of privilege, wealth, and power. Unsystematic and prone to contradiction as it surely is, his literary approach has some distinct advantages. His style melds and personalizes matter that often, in the sages' learned treatises, comes across as abstract, abstruse, and merely academic. He presents uncomfortable truths in comfortable forms, in diatribes leavened by ironic humor, and examines searching ontological and epistemological questions in formats that delight, even as they unsettle readers' complacency. Much of his works' popularity, and his own cult of personality, depends on his tendency to reflect his audiences' underlying skepticism, to anticipate their own dissatisfactions and anxieties in a manner that allows them to acknowledge and affirm them, without requiring too close scrutiny. Readers may, but need not, ponder the implications of his darker propositions.

This is true today just as it was when Twain was first published. His enormous popularity, attested to by his *Autobiography*'s place on the 2011 bestseller lists, is strangely matched by American culture's failure to fully acknowledge the graveness, outrage, and pessimism characterizing so much of his commentary on his homeland and those he called "the damned human race." His works continue to engender evasive misreadings, bowdlerized renditions, and an undeserved reputation for cheerfulness and optimism belied by the texts themselves. Ernest Hemingway's curious endorsement of *Huckleberry Finn* as "the best book we've had" but only if you do not read the final chapters, which he dismissed as "just cheating," illustrates an enduring craving among the novel's readers for happier endings, clearer resolutions, and depictions of a more idealized culture than his writings can ever actually yield. However well-intentioned, censored versions, from the wide range of plays and films of an idyllic relation between Huck, Jim, and Tom to sanitized forthcoming editions of the books that replace the historically significant epithets *nigger* and *Injun* with less offensive terms, distort the works' meanings by diminishing their historical realism and acute social critique. Moreover, they obscure Twain's own blind spots and prejudices, and the vital lessons to be drawn from reflection upon them.

That Twain's major ideas may in places be difficult to tease out is a strength and a weakness of his literary endeavor, especially his fiction. As we have argued previously, the concreteness of fiction, which embodies abstract ideas in specific elements—characters, settings, props, relations—makes such ideas accessible in popular form to a mass audience even as it affords readers a certain shelter from discordant implications. Twain's stories, which frequently dramatize philosophical, psychological, and economic insights, act on audiences at differing levels, partly according to their own receptivity to the message, be it a nostalgic reverie, a tirade against his culture's hypocrisy, or a nuanced depiction of human aspirations and failures. Certainly Twain is not alone among these authors in being misunderstood or misrepresented. Readers also ignorantly or willfully misread Nietzsche, Freud, and Marx; however, misreading is not as fundamental to their continued popularity as it is to Twain's.

Twain's indictments of religion and God, for which a hundred years of churchgoing audiences might have vilified or rejected him, display this ability to teeter on the threshold of the unacceptable, the taboo—which he recognized as having its own special allure. It was the young Mark Twain, after all, who enticed prospective audience members to his lectures with the promise that "the trouble begins at eight." This strategy appears not only in final, published works, but even in some notebook jottings. One aphoristic entry revises Robert Burns's famous lament about man, asserting that "God's inhumanity to man makes countless thousands mourn."[1] Typically literary in style, this rewrite embodies even as it deconstructs the deity, a subversive tactic allowing Twain to draw readers in before they recognize the sacrilege. In order to instill disbelief in a God whose presence is so firmly entrenched in his and others' worldviews, Twain personifies a God unworthy of belief. The God of his upbringing is, for the author, a corrupt mirror of man, and so Twain slyly, elegantly replaces man with him in Robert Burns's saying. The real drama of the line, its anger and despondency, are latent, fully available only with careful reflection, perhaps, but even without it still felt. This embedding of profundities glimpsed but not fully grasped is endemic in Twain's work. In famous scenes like Huck Finn's embracing of hell, a hell that is worthy of a slave liberator, and Satan's questions in the later, more radical *No. 44, The Mysterious Stranger*—about whether a responsible God would blame his human children for sins of his own creation—Twain does not argue directly against faith, but sows doubt and skepticism through settings, situations, and characters his audience identifies with.

The period's dismantling of religious paradigms led our featured writers to reassessments of ethics, and to the realms of conscience, with its dual and dueling burdens of guilt and responsibility. Unlike the materialist Marx, who focuses on phenomena more subject to empirical inquiry, Nietzsche, Freud, and Twain find guilt a compelling subject of study among the powerful, often destructive forces of the human psyche. Guilt is as much a legal as a moral category, and an unpleasant subjective experience framed increasingly in the nineteenth century by psychological rather than narrowly religious considerations. Nietzsche, Freud, and Twain explore both individual and social expressions and consequences of guilt as crucial to understanding human experience. While Marx, in his role as scientist, concentrates on the chain of causation resulting in true and false attributions of responsibility, instead of the psychological mechanisms and manifestations of guilt, he similarly spills much ink over the trouble humans have grasping right, rights, and wrong. He too looks at the odd distortions of consciousness arising from what he argues is a misapprehension of the real relations between people, and between producers and what they produce. His conceptions of alienation, fetishization, the myth of primitive accumulation, and ideology converge in their dependence on people's misapprehension of their responsibility—their true causal relation— to the conditions of their lives. Each author seeks to throw off the burdens of guilt—through understanding its psychological roots in irresistible psychic and cultural forces, rejecting responsibility through nihilistic solipsism, or, in Marx's case, setting up a new, just socioeconomic system no longer dependent on myth, exploitive practices, and arbitrary hierarchies.

All of our writers resist conventional morality. They stand against and seek to disrupt systems—political, religious, philosophical— that organize the world around a binary of good and evil. Marx's rejection of a division between diligent, intelligent owners and lazy, witless laborers shares with Freud's theories of the struggle between the superego and the id a belief in more complex and nuanced evaluations of human behavior. While opposing customary assignments of good and evil, all four writers nonetheless pursue human improvement; their projects venture to reassess and redefine these oversimplified terms. Sharing the reformer's impulse with varying degrees of zeal, each seeks to find a better *good*, to fashion a better human society.

Our authors often look to the past for models of the better society, the better people they wish to see, imagining the constraints of civilization as a profound source of human misery. They look, in typical nineteenth- and early twentieth-century fashion, to "primitive" peoples, often tribal groups whose social organizations and customs differ from theirs, to imagine some "earlier" state holding clues to man's true nature and natural social life. This is less a measure of respect for those peoples than an indictment of the trend of contemporary politics and culture, a repudiation of the popular, widespread affirmation of human progress. Each refutes the notion that chronological progress is necessarily aligned with human advancement. Even Marx, the only one of the four whose view assumes that positive progress both can and will be made, predicts it only conditionally as a result of improvements in education, continuing enlightenment, and constant struggle.

The theme and trope of human slavery is among the most crucial of human struggles, one Twain, Nietzsche, Freud, and Marx all gravitate toward and ruminate on. This is unsurprising, given the period's real and figurative battles against its literal forms and its virtual reappearance in new types of labor throughout the United States and the world. They probe our enslavement to multiple disparate entities, both external forces—like culture, ideology, and the very tangible shackle—and internal ones, psychological and spiritual forces shaping our fates. They raise questions and advance theories about human bondage and autonomy, self-determination, and will. All call for a greater, broader realm of human freedom, for liberty from the constraints that they have worked so hard to identify, the chains imposed on us or wrought by us.

Mark Twain is certainly a jester, and a very great one. As America's foremost humorist, he has earned our admiration for his wit, gentle or barbed. But we contend that he is also a sage, though of a different breed than his esteemed contemporaries. His works, less rigorous but more accessible and entertaining than theirs, have amply rewarded our comparative inquiry. Read lightly, Twain amuses and entertains as none of the sages can. Read deeply and carefully, he provokes, challenges, and enlightens, just as they do.

NOTES

1. From Twain's notebook for 1895, as cited in Henry Nash Smith, *Mark Twain: The Development of a Writer* (Cambridge: Harvard University Press, 1962), 203.

Works Cited

Ball, Terence. "History: Critique and Irony." In *The Cambridge Companion to Marx,* ed. Terrell Carver. New York: Cambridge University Press, 1991.

Barnett, Vincent. *Marx.* London: Routledge, 2009.

Carver, Terrell, ed. *The Cambridge Companion to Marx.* New York: Cambridge University Press, 1991.

Freud, Sigmund. *The Standard Edition of the Complete Psychological Works of Sigmund Freud.* 24 vols. London: Hogarth Press, 1962–1966.

Hill, Hamlin. *Mark Twain God's Fool.* New York: Harper and Row, 1973.

Howells, William Dean. "My Mark Twain." In *Literary Friends and Acquaintances,* ed. David F. Hiatt and Edwin H. Cady. Bloomington: Indiana University Press, 1968. Kaplan, Justin. *Mr. Clemens and Mark Twain.* New York: Simon and Schuster, 1966.

Krass, Peter. *Ignorance, Confidence and Filthy Rich Friends.* Hoboken: Wiley and Sons, 2007.

Lears, T. J. Jackson. *Fables of Abundance.* New York: HarperCollins, 1994.

———. *No Place of Grace.* New York: Pantheon Books, 1981.

Loving, Jerome. *Mark Twain: The Adventures of Samuel L. Clemens.* Berkeley: University of California Press, 2010.

Marx, Karl. *Capital.* Vol. 1. New York: Random House, 1977.

Marx, Karl, and Friedrich Engels. *The Marx-Engels Reader.* Ed. Robert C. Tucker. New York: Norton, 1978.

McLellan, David. *Karl Marx: His Life and Thought.* New York: Harper, 1973.

McMurtry, John. *The Structure of Marx's World-View.* Princeton: Princeton University Press, 1978.

Miller, Richard W. "Social and Political Theory: Class, State, Revolution." In *The Cambridge Companion to Marx,* ed. Terrell Carver. New York: Cambridge University Press, 1991.

Nietzsche, Friedrich. *The Genealogy of Morals.* Trans. Francis Golffing. Garden City: Doubleday, 1956.

Paine, Albert Bigelow. *Mark Twain: A Biography.* 4 vols. New York: Harper and Brothers, 1912.

Reiman, Jeffrey. "Moral Philosophy: The Critique of Capitalism and the Problem of Ideology." In *The Cambridge Companion to Marx,* ed. Terrell Carver. New York: Cambridge University Press, 1991.

Robinson, Forrest G. "An 'Unconscious and Profitable Cerebration': Mark Twain and Literary Intentionality." *Nineteenth-Century Literature* 5 (1995): 357–80.

Salomon, Roger B. *Twain and the Image of History.* New Haven: Yale University Press, 1961.

Sattelmeyer, Robert, and Joseph Donald Crowley, eds. *One Hundred Years of Huckleberry Finn: The Boy, His Book, and American Culture: Centennial Essays.* Columbia: University of Missouri Press, 1985.

Smith, Janet, ed. *Mark Twain on the Damned Human Race.* New York: Hill and Wang, 1962.

Taylor, Paul. "The Education of a Young Capitalist." In *One Hundred Years of Huckleberry Finn: The Boy, His Book, and American Culture: Centennial Essays,* ed. Robert Sattelmeyer and Joseph Donald Crowley. Columbia: University of Missouri Press, 1985.

Trachtenberg, Alan. *The Incorporation of America.* New York: Hill and Wang, 1982.

Twain, Mark. *Adventures of Huckleberry Finn*. Berkeley: University of California Press, 1985.

———. *The Adventures of Tom Sawyer*. The Oxford Mark Twain. New York: Oxford University Press, 1996.

———. *The Autobiography of Mark Twain*. Ed. Charles Neider. New York: Harper and Brothers, 1959.

———. *Collected Tales, Sketches, Speeches, and Essays*. 2 vols. New York: The Library of America, 1992.

———. *A Connecticut Yankee in King Arthur's Court*. The Oxford Mark Twain. New York: Oxford University Press, 1996.

———. *Following the Equator*. The Oxford Mark Twain. New York: Oxford University Press, 1996.

———. *Life on the Mississippi*. The Oxford Mark Twain. New York: Oxford University Press, 1996.

———. "The Man That Corrupted Hadleyburg." In *Great Short Works of Mark Twain*. New York: Harper and Row, 1967.

———. *Mark Twain–Howells Letters*. 2 vols. Ed. Henry Nash Smith and William M. Gibson. Cambridge: Harvard University Press, 1960.

———. *Mark Twain's Notebook*. Ed. Albert Bigelow Paine. New York: Harper and Brothers, 1935.

———. Mark Twain Papers. Bancroft Library, University of California, Berkeley.

———. *The Mysterious Stranger*. Ed. William M. Gibson. Berkeley: University of California Press, 1969.

———. *The Prince and the Pauper*. The Oxford Mark Twain. New York: Oxford University Press, 1996.

———. *Pudd'nhead Wilson and Those Extraordinary Twins*. Ed. Sidney E. Berger. New York: Norton, 2005.

———. *Roughing It*. The Oxford Mark Twain. New York: Oxford University Press, 1996.

———. *What Is Man? and Other Philosophical Writings*. Ed. Paul Baender. Berkeley: University of California Press, 1973.

Index